MIDLIFE
ILLNESS
TOUR

BASED ON A MEMOIR

By Elise Kaye

A message from the author

After writing a daily blog on my travels throughout Asia in 2017-2018 I wanted to tell a down to earth story. I wanted it to appeal to the everyday person, the person who isn't a traveller or adventurer.
I wanted it to inspire women and men who were going through divorce ,separation,grief or turmoil.to get up and do something different,to provide a guide to kick start their lives again.

Although many events did happen some of the story involves artistic licensing to provide an entertaining story.

I hope you enjoy the sentiment.

peter,
Thanks for
being my world
buddy
Wae

For Elena
My rock, my reason for being

PROLOGUE

DREAMS

From an early age, I always had vivid dreams - my best ideas would come to me when dreaming.

I loved to sleep and dream up creative adventures as I drifted off into a colourful hypnotic state. I slept in the afternoon, I slept at night, I'd wake up and go back to sleep again. I just loved to sleep.

Travel would always feature in my dreams and I would be the flung across the globe into far reaching countries – usually having some scary and surreal experiences. I think my love of travel came to me at an early age and it was surprising to me that I hadn't opted to live and settle abroad. A re-occurring dream about a giant shipwreck on an island was one of my favourites. It was a large grey ship with grand white sails like the ones featured in eighteenth-century paintings.

I had very lovely dreams. Being a wistful child, I also spent my days dreaming, mainly to escape the monotony of living in a sleepy mining village in Yorkshire. Calling the village sleepy was being kind - the village was dead. There was more life in the cemetery than amongst the community. The brave one's got out and moved away but I stayed for a while - until love eventually pulled me further south.

I was going to be something: I couldn't be just stuck there. I yearned to be an actress and I liked being the centre of attention. I wanted to run away, and spent my whole life running away and trying to find 'my people'.

In my adult years, the dreams had dissipated. I made friends with insomnia and interrupted sleep, mainly brought on by stress and excessive alcohol consumption. A few gin and tonics here and there were never any good for creativity. My overzealous, over conscious, but slightly adult brain interrupted any excitement I was having, like a realistic meteorite crashing down to earth.

4

As a child, I wrote poetry. I filled books with the words I'd made up in my slumber and always kept a notebook by my bed. My favourite notebook was purple, hard backed, and bought from Woolworths - long before it was taken into administration and a piece of my childhood was crushed forever.

As I hit my twenties, I got out of the habit of writing and eventually stopped altogether; meeting boys and going out seemed far more important to my twenty-one-year-old self.

The dreams never went away. I forgot most of them over the years, but there were two poignant ones that left an imprint on my brain I couldn't shake off.

My first significant dream happened in 2003. At the time I was living with a very jealous and possessive boyfriend who had far too much testosterone. When he would follow me to the shops I would daydream and imagine I was somewhere else. I used my dreams to escape his physical abuse. It made everything more bearable.

I also convinced myself that I had some form of spiritual gift.

My dream was set in a dusty battlefield which looked like the Middle East, it could have easily been Iraq or Afghanistan. There was nothing but arid land and army camps. It lacked colour like a sepia photograph: lots of brown and greys settled underneath the stifling hot and hazy sun. My throat was dry from inhaling dust and concrete and my body was aching. In my hand I carried a rifle, which weighed down my small body.

There were bodies piled up. Scores of corpses piled up with white and khaki dust sheets covering them. I wasn't alarmed by this. Something told me I was immune to seeing them, like it was a daily occurrence.

I was serving alongside a man. A beautiful man around 5 foot and 10 inches tall. He was in his late twenties and dressed in Khaki.

His eyes were hazel but shone bright green against the sun. His smile was beautiful. Cheeky and naughty but very, very beautiful. His eyes were beguiling, like a hundred souls had owned those eyes and I'd been by his side in the life of every soul. I felt at ease with him.

5

We didn't just communicate through speech, or even through our body language. I could look into his eyes and instantly fall deep into a daze.

All of a sudden, I heard a gunshot.

Someone had aggressively opened fire and I was immediately frightened. I was shot in the leg and fell to the ground in pain. I was taken by ambulance to a hospital and placed on a bed in a white room. The room was drip white with a mechanical looking metal bed with white PVC covering. I was scared, frightened, and I wanted to go home. My heart was racing with fear.

The green-eyed man appeared again, but this time he wasn't a soldier - he was a Doctor. He smiled at me and told me I was going to be just fine as drifted in and out of woozy consciousness. I don't remember any more of the dream, but I remember waking up back in my room in Yorkshire next to my horrible boyfriend. I woke disorientated and taken aback. The dream stayed with me and played on my mind. I didn't understand why.

I brushed this off as watching too much news at the time - it was 2003 after all and there was an emerging war developing in the Middle East.

The second significant dream I had was in another foreign land. I'd moved to Staffordshire at this point and replaced one miserable mining village for another, all in the name of love.

This dream was set in a cold land. I was a mother and had lots of children. Many, many children. They were dressed in stark clothing but were very smiley - poor but pleasantly happy. I wasn't dressed in stark clothing; my clothes were beautiful. A long white chiffon dress with an almost angelic like cloak.

I hadn't yet considered having children before this dream occurred in 2004, and certainly wouldn't have pictured myself wearing white. Short skirts, revealing vest tops, and stilettos would have been my fashion choice at the time.

In the dream, we lived by a mass of water surrounded by mountains, where I swam in the cold lake every day. Every time I came out of the

6

lake, I emerged like a goddess; happier and more serene. My cloak turned silver, and more children would appear. By the time the dream had ended I had multiple children, smiley, happy, giggly children.

I believe the mind is a funny thing. It can do all sorts of things, most of which can't be explained. Water and sun have always had a calming effect on me.

I didn't realise the significance of these dreams until many years later. It took my midlife illness to gain clarity.

Chapter 1
Birmingham airport, UK , Christmas Day 2017

Dark clouds enveloped the sky over Birmingham. It was a miserable, cold, and slightly depressing day - the type of day that should be trade-marked and branded U.K. weather.

I dropped my car off at the on-site car park and headed towards the terminal building. I walked slowly then built up speed as the rain drenched me to the bone, my shoes squelching as I walked.

My long dark hair annoying flapped around and across my face, smudging my bright red lipstick across my mouth and cheeks. I now resembled a sad old clown after a night on the tiles. Apart from the lipstick, I was bare faced. The world wasn't quite ready to have my unmade face unleashed upon it, and I wasn't brave enough to try. At just over 40 years old I was realistic. I was gradually coming to terms with aging and no longer felt like the vibrant youthful beauty I'd once been. But I was okay with it, I could turn the odd head still.

I wasn't used to the weight of the heavy green backpack clinging to my back - it was so uncomfortable. Standing at 5ft 4inches tall, the bag was almost as big as me. As I staggered slowly, my back twisted and slightly tilted to the side. I felt as if I was anticipating a fall that could happen at any time.

Seeing as I would be carrying this around for the next month, I would need to toughen up and see it as a good workout. I wrestled to tip it to one side, trying to secure it to my back.

A backpack wasn't my usual style choice but nor were the walking boots, leggings, and hoodie I was wearing - I was more of a Samsonite and Mulberry handbag sort of a girl. I was someone who always boarded a plane looking like I should be working as a glamourous air stewardess serving coffee, not traveling on it.

Under normal circumstances I would fly fully made up wearing stylish clothes and heels. I lived in constant fear of what people would think of me, this stemmed from having a Mother with high expectations. I think psychologists refer to this as the critical parent tape being played time after time. I never felt good enough.

"Put some lipstick on and brighten your face up", she'd said from as soon as I hit puberty.
"Cover up that acne, no one wants to see your spots", she'd criticise.

I was made to feel as if my appearance would reflect badly on her. Years and years of being criticised with jealous taunts meant my relationship with her was now non-existent.

I gingerly stepped through the revolving doors - almost caving under the weight of my bag - and stumbled into the departures area. It was familiar territory but this time I wasn't there for business or a family holiday.
I took in a deep breath.
As I exhaled, I thought about how this was a far cry from the all-inclusive Caribbean and Indian Ocean trips I'd taken in the past.
How there was no business class lounge or Emirates driver picking me up from home and hand delivering me to the door.
I thought about my previous job and those types of holidays.
My heart sank with joylessness.
They had served me well at the time, but after one or two Eat-All-You-Want buffets, being treated like a corporate queen, and having Margaritas and Pina Coladas on tap - what else was there to do in such circumstances? I was relieved those days were behind me.
I needed coffee. This was going to be a very long and emotionally draining day. I was going to be spending a lot of time alone, and that wasn't always a good thing.

"Table for one please," I said as I was gently ushered to the booth in Frankie Benny's. "I'm only having coffee; will that be ok?" I asked apologetically - not wanting to take up the table of potentially more worthy food purchasers.
"It's fine, we are very quiet this afternoon," replied the sweet, petite, blonde waitress.

9

I sat back with my head resting against red padded seat, gulping my coffee and watching people coming and going through the revolving doors, as I had a moment before. I was imagining all sorts of scenarios and started to relax as I sipped the smooth, bitter taste of the filtered coffee. My imagination was my talent. A talent that had sometimes got me into trouble. A talent that had enabled me to be a part time stage performer, part time fraud.

I sat and observed two beautifully dressed red headed children, sat on their animal designed Trunkie luggage, whizzing along the floor. It looked like a competitive race between brother and sister. The boy had obviously won and began shouting;

"I'm the winner and you're the loser, you're such a loser!" making an L shape with his fingers, putting them to his head, and mocking his sister.

The sister, not wanting her brother to get the upper hand, said;

"Let's see, let's have another race and I'll beat you this time!"

As I watched the sweet pair of siblings, a warm wave of nostalgia hit my heart and ran across my chest and down into my legs. I strained a smile and clenched my jaw to prevent myself welling up. I didn't want to cry, I tried my best not to, but so many things set me off nowadays. I was a perpetual blarter, crying my eyes out at anything.

At the far side of the airport by the check-in desks was a woman, possibly their Mum, busily organising everyone. Checking passports, insurance documents, and boarding passes for various family members.

For a moment, I wished that was me. I wanted to be the organising Mum, making sure my family were okay and stressing about the holiday. I wanted to be the bossy mum, straightening her children's clothes and making sure her parents were okay too. I'd never been a bossy anything; which felt like a shame. Inside me was a stubborn bossy woman desperate to get out.

I spotted an elderly Indian couple heading towards the desks, laden down with multiple suitcases and bags whilst being hugged by - what I presumed were - their daughters and grandchildren. They looked so frail and I wondered how they'd cope when they landed at their destination. 'I could always help them if they were on my flight' I thought, aiming to get into the 'helping' mindset. A mindset that would serve me well on this journey.

I envied the families who did everything together. I'd never had a big family holiday with grandparents, parents, and children, but I took comfort in knowing the reality of such situations were less than perfect. My family were great, but we were all so different that such a trip would never have worked.

Since becoming an international airport, Birmingham had far more exciting flights than your run of the mill trip to Tenerife. It wasn't unusual to see a variety of people heading to Delhi, Mumbai, Dubai, and Istanbul. Birmingham airport is small and easy to navigate - unlike Heathrow which gave me a panic attack just to think about.

"I suppose not many people choose to go away Christmas Day," I said, trying to make conversation with the waitress, unsure of when I'd next get to chat to someone.

"We were busier earlier, loads of flights to Alicante and The Canaries going out," the waitress sighed. "We had a lot of kids in this morning, they were noisy and made a right mess, bloody pain in the arse they were!" she said as she turned her lip up, seemingly not happy about it.

I imagined most people would be at home on Christmas Day with their families, playing games, watching the Queen's speech, and falling asleep in a deep sleepy coma induced by excessive food and alcohol. I longed for a Christmas Day like that. I longed to cook the dinner for a big group of loved ones, drink a rich smooth glass of fruity Malbec, and curl up on the sofa with my loving family. Growing up, Christmas had been fun to a point. My Gran and Grandad always came around, and Mum cooked a big lunch. We got to sit at the posh table and chairs that we were only allowed to sit on at Christmas or for special occasions. We always had three courses and ate beef - Grandad found turkey boring. I'd personally begun to find beef boring after having it for Christmas dinner fifteen years in a row. My mum wasn't the best cook, but it was never about that. It was about us all being together.

Sat in the airport I thought about my Gran, who I'd lost only a few days before, and Grandad, who we'd lost four years ago. My Grandma, the peacekeeper, a sweet and gentle woman.

I got upset. I hadn't seen her for eight years due to family rifts - rifts I had been determined not to create with my own little family when I got married.

Christmas was great when we were little. As we developed into teenagers, it became less enjoyable. Christmas in my early twenties were filled with hangovers and headaches. My brother and I had drinking competitions -which seemed a great idea at the time - but was less fun by lunchtime on Christmas day.

I longed for those days; days when the family were all together.

I longed for a lot of things - sitting alone in an airport on Christmas Day with no one to talk to but a disgruntled waitress was not one of them.

Before I set off, I nipped to have lunch with my friend and her family, but I could feel that my heart wasn't in it. The food was delicious, even if it was vegetarian, and they were all full of Christmas joy. I just wanted to get on the plane and escape. They sensed this as I made my excuses and left for the airport early.

Before I booked to go away, I'd been invited to various friend's homes but declined. Partly to appear the 'woe is me' victim, and partly out of sheer stubbornness.

I was determined not to enjoy Christmas.

I was still angry. Angry that I'd been put in this position and angry at life.

I wanted to be so many things, so many people in many scenarios. One thing I didn't want to be was lonely, but loneliness had been thrust upon me and didn't know what to do.

I longed for my old life. I looked back, seeing how my life could have been if I had been different.

Hindsight does things to you, it creates a beautiful blush tint across the least enjoyable memories of life.

In truth, I didn't know who I was or what I wanted anymore.

Chapter 2
Home life

"Steve, what's happening with this house hunt? We've been talking about it for 12 months, and we haven't looked at one house yet," I shouted from the kitchen as I cooked Sunday morning breakfast. That was a lie. I'd looked at a couple of houses with my friend Kate and reported them back to Steve who, as usual, shrugged off the idea of moving. He'd owned the house about a year before we'd met so had a huge attachment to it. After 12 years in a two-bedroom house, it was time to move. I'd never really had the same affiliation; it never really felt like my home.

The neighbours were great, but since becoming a family we'd outgrown it. Sophia was six at this point and we were bursting at the seams, practically getting on top of each other.

The girls, Sophia, and I were constantly banished to the dining room while Steve watched football in the quiet. He sat in his red and white painted man cave, complete with red leather sofa, that was otherwise known as the living room. It wasn't very feminine or very cosy as a home because Steve had always chosen the décor. I was reassured that once we did eventually move that I could least chose some of the furnishings.

I did sneak the odd cushion or picture frame into the house when Steve worked away. I'd never disrespect his taste though. I'd always compromise as I didn't want to cause conflict.

He was such a 'typical man'. I'd told myself: men like to be in charge of their castle and have things just how they want. I was comfortable living like that if it meant an easy life and a happy husband.

I didn't have a realistic view of men. I'd lived with someone in my twenties and that went disastrously wrong. My dad on the other hand was so bloody brilliant that all other men disappointed me. He was generous, gentle, and caring - he would have sat and watched tv and foregone the football just to be with his girls. He was the type of man I wanted in my life and he never let me down. I sometimes wished he lived a bit nearer so I could spend more time with him.

I served up breakfast and sat next to Steve while he watched match of the day.

"What about this one?", I said, showing him the iPad. "It's a four bed, just up the road in a lovely area. Look at the garden! We could stay there a while. It could be our forever home. We're not getting any younger and to think about the long-term,"

I prattled on like a dog chewing a delicious bone. I was tenacious in my approach to finding a new home.

It was an ideal lifestyle - everyone I knew either had it or wanted it.

I was so desperate to move and longed for a lovely four-bedroom house near Cannock Chase; a beautiful stretch of forest two miles from where we lived. We both worked hard, had good jobs with fantastic salaries, and had outgrown the house we were in - it was becoming claustrophobic. We both worked from home and we were working on top of each other making business calls in stereo. I've got to be honest; I was a bit embarrassed that we were doing well but still living in a two up two down tiny home. It wasn't London and house prices were relatively cheap, we could easily afford a bigger house.

I wanted a house where we could regularly host parties and have family over to stay. I craved that type of lifestyle, any excuse to have people around the house. I liked people and was very sociable.

I once had a party at the house and invited 40 guests from my theatre group – much to the horror of Steve. He sat in the living room and ignored my friends the entire night while we sang show tunes at the top of our voices. It was a rare balmy summer evening, so I wanted to make the most of it with friends. Steve sulked all night and referred to our awful *'din'* disturbing the neighbours. The truth was, one neighbour was old and already in bed and the others were in our garden, enjoying the party.

Steve preferred to lead a simpler life reading the paper and watching TV, usually some form of sport. He had little interest in theatre stuff. In fact, it irritated him, despite him introducing me to the theatre company. One of Steve's friends was a member.

He had the potential to be the life and soul of the party but on his terms, with his friends and work colleagues, and when he was the centre of attention, not me.

At home, he liked to be quiet and not to bring noise into the house.

"I get enough chat at work, I don't want it at home," he'd say.

"This is my house, my rules! A house without rules runs into disarray"

He'd often say this in his calm authoritarian voice, half joking, half serious.

He was always saying I was too noisy and that I didn't stop talking. He liked order and discipline, and I was a bit of a hippy with a weird hybrid personality of a business chick with a carefree attitude to life. Nothing bothered me because I always had a plan B, C and D up my sleeve reserved for when things went wrong. I enjoyed the challenge that change gave me.

Steve meticulously planned every detail of his life so there was no room for error or need for a backup plan. He would never allow himself to get things wrong.

In some instances, we were like chalk and cheese, but we had the same sense of humour, so it worked in so many ways. I needed someone to keep me on the straight and narrow, but Steve required fun. That was the deal, and that was what we both brought to the marriage.

"Steve, will you at least think about it?" I continued badgering him like a 90's timeshare rep from a Spanish resort.

"Yes Babe, we can look another day when I've got time," he answered in a vague voice.

"We've got time, it's Sunday morning and you're just watching T.V."

16

I didn't like Steve's recent vagueness.
Vague was non-committal, vague was indefinite, and vague wasn't me
- nor was it Steve.

"And what about this year's family holiday? Where shall we go?" I
interrupted before he could even get out his speech.

I could hear myself prattling on like some neurotic nag. I was nervous.
Nervous that his behaviour was out of character and too evasive.

"Let's not commit to one this year, babe," he replied.
He never said that, and I knew he'd arranged a lad's trip for later in
the year.

'Maybe he was going to surprise me with a trip away somewhere?
Maybe he'd asked my dad to babysit for a few nights so we could go
away?' I told myself in anticipation.
Although, he wasn't great at booking holidays and he never did
surprises. He'd once booked a trip to Devon that he'd left until the last
minute. We ended up in a home for elderly people with special needs
and it had totally put me off Devon for a few years.
We'd travelled all over; Mauritius, Morocco, Italy, India, San
Francisco, New York - the list was endless. He loved a holiday: we
both enjoyed a holiday together. It was our thing - or maybe looking
back maybe it was 'my' thing, and he just went along with it.
Come to think of it, he'd not done much travelling before we met. I'd
lived in Italy and been away a lot as a child.
Perhaps he was just happy to stay at home and go to the pub with the
lads. That wasn't Steve's style to go along with things though. He was
an uncompromising type of guy, strong and stubborn, and that's why
I liked him. I'm a little bit stubborn and it's a quality I find admirable
in people. I'm drawn to stubbornness like a moth to a light. I like
strong people; I find it charming. I couldn't be with a man who let me

do everything and had no power or opinion, it would bore the life out of me.

We'd always been a team, we had to be. We both worked so many hours that we had to make it work. We were team 'Kaye', and it all worked just fine - even if we often spent weeks where we barely saw each other. I'd spent an entire summer up in Leeds with Sophia because I was working up there. It made sense as my Dad was up there to babysit.
I thought this was normal suburban life - wasn't it? We'd never had a relationship where we lived in each other's pockets. I would have hated it; and so would he. We had our own lives and we were both fiercely independent people. Two alphas stamping our own personalities on the world and doing a damn great job of it.

"Winter weekends are for sports, babe," he'd say in his pseudo posh accent mixed with a hint black country.

My friend had joked;
"Where the hell does his posh accent come from? He doesn't sound like anyone from around here,"

"I don't know. I like it, it makes him sound educated and don't like stupid men," I replied.

Maybe he put it on to make himself appear grander and well read, or perhaps it was to hide his real roots. His real roots were more grounded, more earthy, and a bit rough and ready.
He'd dip in and out of family time when it suited him, but I didn't mind.
His family weren't particularly close and never had parties or socialised with each other - something I thought was odd when we first met. I was from a family of no secrets, where we went out together, were always at each other's houses, and consulted each other

18

on all aspects of our lives. My family gave me space to be myself but were there when I needed them.

His family were at each other's throats; just a bunch of people thrown together by genetics without a care or thought for each other. They worked against each other rather than with. I had my Dad and Brother, and load of Cousins, Aunties and Uncles all there to help me out. They might have been 130 miles away, but we were close. I felt sorry for him not having the type of family I did, I was lucky. My family was his family, and my Grandad loved him. Dad was less enamoured, but that's only because I was his little girl. The female members of my family found him charming, and he was a charmer.

We'd been together a long time and I was beginning to sound like a nag; the type of wife I hated. The school mums demanding two or three holidays a year, bigger houses, Range Rovers, and gym memberships, all while they sat at home doing nothing and expecting husbands to pay. This was a slight on some of the school mums. I gravitated to the workers, the non-demanding ones who paid their own way. I admired the ones rushing out the door, juggling toast and kids while taking a business call. The modern mums who just got on with things and set their own expectations.
I was chilled. I contributed equally to the household and used my bonuses towards paying off the decreasing mortgage. I paid for my own gym membership, and sometimes worked a 60-hour week to ensure we had enough to save for a new house.

He'd recently remarked,
"You're always working, always away, why can't you be a typical wife? All you ever talk about is bloody work, you're becoming a work bore, and I hate it."
I was 'Miss Career Girl'. I hadn't quite achieved what I wanted to, so I pushed myself further. I wanted Steve to be proud of me, to notice I was good.

I didn't have time for cleaning; we had someone in to do that. I didn't iron either; we took our things to the ironing shop, and most weeks I was always too tired cook – although when I did, it was always a fantastic meal.

Life just rolled like that in the Kaye household and it suited us fine. Life outside work was for living, for travelling, eating out, and for being with friends - not for doing household chores and watching TV. Maybe I did talk about work a lot, but it was a big part of my life and part of the way things were. My job was good, I was good at it, and I worked hard. It also meant we had no money worries like most couples, and rarely spoke a crossed word about money – or anything else. I was happy with my lot and relaxed with my relationship with Steve.

Our wedding was beautiful and took place in Alghero on the island of Sardinia. It was a little bit glamorous and we chartered a boat to take guests to the reception. I designed my silver tulle wedding dress, and the photos were stunning – I felt like a Disney princess.

People talked about it for years afterwards. The sun shone, and we both glowed with happiness.

We both had style and class when it came to clothes, food, and – of course – wedding venues. The wedding summed us up. A classy couple with impeccable taste. I liked nice things, and so did he, but I was equally happy to do the basics like camping. Steve hated camping, he hated basic.

My home was my sanctuary. My family time and our marriage were sacred. I loved my daughter and my husband more than anything in the world, and we had a great life.

Some people were envious of our lifestyle – even a bit jealous. We always did our own thing but came together when it mattered and always supported each other on decisions with Sophia. She was, and always will be, our world.

Neither of us were particularly uneasy on the eye, although, I was getter a few cracks around the eyes. But nothing that a bit of Botox couldn't sort.

There had been lots of opportunities for me to stray, and I knew people found Steve very attractive - he must have had ample opportunity to. But I trusted him, and I would gush to all my friends about how he didn't find other women attractive; he only had eyes for me. I was so comfortable in my skin I didn't care about his 'admirers'. He loved the attention, so I let him lap it up, as I did. But we had each other, and in my eyes, that was all that mattered.

We were so in love, no one else mattered.

Only a fool would want to give up what we had.

Chapter 3
Back at Birmingham airport

I hurled my backpack up onto my back and headed towards the check-in desks.

As I quickly approached the escalator my feet felt unsteady. I wobbled from side to side aiming to get my balance – I could feel myself tilting to one side and almost falling on the guy in front of me.

A sweet looking couple in their twenties dived in to prop me up. The guy put his hand under my armpit – as I wondered if I'd showered sufficiently enough – he lifted me slightly while his girlfriend held my shoulder. I was more embarrassed at the sweat pouring out of my pits and whether he could hold my weight than about actually falling over. I felt like a silly old lady. This travelling halfway around the world was clearly not for me. I should have stuck to a package tour and a suitcase.

I was thankful I was in Birmingham and Brummies are a friendly lot. If this had been London or any other big city in the world I would have fallen flat on my face while hundreds of people either trampled across me, walked around me, or ignored the fact I even existed. I was used to feeling invisible though, I'd felt invisible in social settings for a long time.

Once I'd hit my late thirties, I had this wonderful superpower called invisibility. I knew the power got stronger with age. My purpose in life had happened, I'd been married and had Sophia. There was nothing else I could offer the world.

Except, I had this feeling, this yearning that my life hadn't started at all, like I'd been rehearsing for the last few years. There was a massive crescendo performance yet to happen, only I didn't know what.

I dragged my aching back towards check in, desperate to get rid of the twenty-kilogram weight I had strapped to my back.

The check in desk was fairly quiet. I dropped off the backpack, grateful to get rid of it. I could still feel the indentations that had tunnelled into my skin and my shoulders were red and bumpy.

Left with only a small grey bum bag containing money, phone, cards, and passport, I was liberated for the first time that day, knowing the next time I'd see that dreaded ruck sack would be in Delhi. Delhi would be busy, and I'd need my wits about me to survive even the airport.

It had been a long time since I'd last been to Delhi, but I knew it was hectic. Recent horror stories of solo female travellers in India hadn't help to ease my troubled mind. I knew when I arrived, there would be crowds of faces holding up boards with various poor spellings of European surnames such as 'Mr Smit' and my favourite, 'Mr Jone'.

I headed through security and was told to take off my heavy walking boots and put them in the tray. My boots were new – in fact, brand new – Dad had bought me them for Christmas and I'd unwrapped the present that morning hoping for a more elaborate gift. A nice pair of heels or a make-up set. Dad being practical as ever had thought I needed walking boots for my trip.

I did – I just didn't really want them as a gift.

What an ungrateful daughter I was.

Despite wearing fuss free clothing, I still managed to set off the alarms in security and I couldn't even blame my walking boots. How could Lycra leggings, a hoodie, and socks set off the bloody alarms? I convinced myself that this was a ploy by the airport staff to get me a bit more disgruntled before my flight.

Flying in recent years had become a pain as security was ramped up. I wasn't stupid, I knew this was for my own safety, but I'm not renowned for my patience. Waiting too long stressed me out, and I seemed to be in a constant state of stress nowadays. A day without negative body buzz was strange – it was a sensation I'd gotten used to having.

I walked straight through duty free and sat on a bench thinking about what a great morning it had been. I'd woken Sophia around 7am because Santa Claus had been.

I kissed her chubby, rosy cheeks and gently woke her saying, "I wonder if he's been," then we both crept quietly downstairs, anticipating the delights the big man in the red suit had brought.

He'd gone a little bit crazy this year in overcompensation for Mummy not being around much. Santa was feeling very, very guilty on behalf of Mummy, and Mummy paid the price, emotionally and financially. Her eyes lit up with joy as she unwrapped the first present, "Wow mummy, how did he know I wanted a camera? I can vlog now," she said.

I was up to date with the latest trends and new exactly about the craze for Vlogging and YouTube. The opportunist in me also knew there was potential money to be made from it providing we picked a popular topic or genre.

"I love these mummy, say thank you to Santa Claus," she gushed in between nibbling on chocolate as she opened a new pair of dance shoes.

Then she ran into the living room:

"OMG Mom he bought me a bike!" she screamed with excitement.

By 'he' she meant Santa Claus. Santa Claus had been the hero, the benefactor of Christmas. She didn't need to know that I'd taken out a loan to pay for it all as well as for my trip abroad.

I was happy because she was happy, although Christmas for me wasn't an enjoyable experience.

I enjoyed playing the part of Mummy. I enjoyed surprising her, but Christmas for me was a boring series of rituals repeated year after year. I hadn't enjoyed Christmas much beyond the age of 16 and couldn't understand the excitement people had for it. There were a lot of things I couldn't understand in other people, like the excitement of getting home from work to watch their favourite soap, or the joys of binge watching a box set and spending holidays doing the same things. Or gardening. Gardening is chore to me, a boring repetitive chore much like cleaning. It's a maintenance job.

It was all a bit sedentary for me – a bit mind numbing.

When all the presents had been opened, we went through the rigmarole of calling Grandad and various Great Aunts to thank them for their presents.

We ate scrambled egg on toast, and I had small glass of Prosecco knowing that in a few hours' time I'd be driving to the airport and getting out of the country, out of the continent, and out of civilisation.

Back in the airport and I found a seat in the corner of Wetherspoons and ordered a beer. You can't beat 'Spoons for a cheap beer and a cheap meal.

My beer felt like ice cold nectar flowing down my throat as I drank it. My relationship with alcohol was getting better and I was being more adult about my pre-flight consumption. A 5am pre-flight tipple had been my routine when holidaying in the past. I'd get on the plane and have good sleep, then land in resort and start again.

I picked up my phone and looked at it for minute, scanning the photos from the morning's festivities.

I looked at a number in my phone, a special number and sent a text;

'Just a quick note to say Merry Christmas before I go off and find myself in a foreign land'.

I didn't really expect a response from the text's recipient. This person wasn't renowned for being attentive or for any sort of prompt reply – the record for the longest time waiting for a response had been 12 weeks.

Texting and drinking and alcohol had become a habit I had gotten into lately, and this recipient in particular had more than a fair few from me including my favourite drunken 'wanker' texts.

Within seconds I received a message back;

'Hey Beaut, have the best time and we'll catch up when you get back'.

I resisted the temptation to message back. I'd failed so many times before to resist a double or even treble text, and I was no stranger to the occasional quadruple text.

The quadruple text was the defeat of any desperate woman.

Maybe resistance and patience were the new me, a serene and calmer Elise Kaye.

I think I liked it.

I snapped out of my daydream and wandered around the shops in the airport, waiting for the flight to Dubai to be announced. My first of three flights that would take me to my final destination on this trip.

Chapter 4
Problems

Steve and I were growing old together but kept our own sparky individual outlook on life. He was more serious than me, and everything had to be planned and sorted in advance. I was happy to go with the flow, providing my secure family life was there when I needed it. I needed security, someone to come home to when I'd had a bad day at work or travelled away, someone to bounce ideas off and listen to my moans.

Without a base, I was restless and unhinged. My life without security or purpose was manic and uncontrollable. I loved change as long as I had a fall-back plan should it all go wrong.

I'd put on a bit of weight and probably drank more than I used to. It was a combination of boredom and working long hours.

Living in the Staffordshire suburbs is hardly a buzzing lifestyle. Most people I knew drank every night, mainly due to the relentless tedium of their lives. I had a different life to most people I knew and not much in common with the locals. I was creative, career-minded, a Mum, and travel junkie. I needed to be kept active and entertained all the time. Something which is a flaw in me, or so I was told. I needed constant challenge and stimulation – like a child with ADHD and ten tubes of smarties inside them. I was bouncy and fun.

I worked across Europe and the Middle East and spent ten-day stretches in Dubai working as a learning consultant. I'd fly business class and eat in the best restaurants. I was in a theatre group, had singing lessons, went to the gym, and taught drama. I was sure the neighbours thought I was odd some enigma. Maybe that was my overactive imagination and pumped up ego thinking that. Having Sophia eased off some of the hobbies and I opted for more nights at home to get a balanced family life.

Steve played cricket and there was no compromise when it came to that sport – we couldn't go away during the 6-month cricket season. He also supported Manchester United and spent many winter days in

27

the pub watching any televised games. He also went on lot of corporate days to the Rugby, Football, Cricket, dinners, awards, and ceremonies all in the name of entertaining clients.

We had separate hobbies, even lives to some extent, and I never considered this unusual. We'd done it for so long and it suited us.

Our daughter Sophia was our glue. Sassy, intelligent, and the most hilarious child I've ever met, let alone produced and cultivated. Her sense of humour and whit would rival any savvy adult. I don't think she's ever been a child in the usual sense. She spent so much time with adults that she was able to converse and joke with them on a level I'd not seen in a child – but without ever being precocious or annoying. I adored kissing her little chubby face and gazing into her beautiful hazel eyes, touching her soft olive skin and brushing her light brown hair. Such a bloody beautiful and gorgeous child. Steve and I had produced a great kid.

I'd noticed Steve becoming more secretive and hiding his phone. I'd started working nearer to home so I was around a lot more in the evenings. I told myself he'd always kept his phone hidden from view and needed quiet to make phone calls. He often worked late and saw business and social activities as interlinked.

Sophia and I were noisy and always singing and dancing, always messing around and being loud and laughing.

Once Sophia had gone to bed the evenings dragged on. The monotony and repetitive nature of married life wasn't pleasant. Half watching T.V, half thinking about work whilst opening a bottle of wine and sitting in silence. When I didn't have hobbies, I'd often go to bed at 8.30 to relieve the boredom and make the next day come more quickly.

The next day, a day of work. Somewhere I could chat and make a difference, somewhere I felt appreciated. It slowly became my new sanctuary away from the tedium of married life. We were ready for our next move, a move would give us a project to work on together.

This would provide us with purpose and focus and bring back the spark we seemed to be losing.

Steve just wasn't responding anymore.

I thought about the days when we first got together and it made me sad, sad and angry.

"For God's sake Steve what is the matter?' Why can't you see the Doctor? Are you dying and you don't want to tell me?" I bellowed at him, mainly out of frustration.

"Can someone please bring back my husband? I think he's died!" I dramatized, feeling a little mentally unstable.

"Have you got Dementia too? I'll support you, babe, you know I will. I'll stay with you until you give your last breath, I love you!" I said whining and pleading with him to open up.

My desperation was becoming ridiculous and annoying as I clung on to my husband for dear life.

Monday morning came and I booked an appointment for Steve to see the Doctor.

"I've booked an appointment for you Steve, at least let's try to get to the bottom of this," I begged in miserable desperation.

"I'm not going to the Doctors, and I'm not going to work today either," Steve slurred, almost unable to get his words out.

This was unlike him, he loved work and he liked going to the Doctor. Our Doctor was great, and Steve hated letting illness linger so was always willing to go and get things sorted.

"What are you going to do? Sit around dragging your feet and feeling sorry for yourself?" I snapped back worried I'd gone too far.

I was always worried I'd go too far.

Chapter 5
The Journey

It was almost time to board my flight to Dubai. This trip was a 3 stop wonder Birmingham to Dubai, Dubai to Delhi, then Delhi to Kathmandu.
As my departure neared, I became anxious and was already missing Sophia.

What was she doing?
What did she have for her Christmas lunch?
Was she happy or feeling overwhelmed by the events that led up to Christmas?

No mum should be wondering what their small child is doing Christmas Day, they should be with them eating turkey and pulling crackers, playing games like Pie Face or Cluedo.
I re-lived last year's trip to Lapland and how we'd been so happy.
Life had changed, but I still had optimism. I hadn't let events spoil our trip and everything had seemed better with the Elves, Snowflakes, and Christmas cake, which ironically had been the names of some of the elf helpers.

The words of the school mums swam around in my head;

'You haven't thought about your child, why would any mum go away Christmas Day?'

'What the hell are you thinking? You selfish cow.'

'Well I'd never leave my child, especially not at Christmas'.

Going away wasn't indication of how little I cared, quite the opposite. If I'd have stuck around, I would surely have ruined Christmas for everyone.

30

Pangs of guilt hit me, but I didn't want to live the next few years fleeting between feelings of parent guilt coupled with my strong desire to get away and do something exciting.

Going away, in my head, made me a better parent. I hoped that one day Sophia would see this and be proud of me.

You have a child, and suddenly all the things you wanted and who you were before disappear. As you become a parent, all the things you wanted to do before become secondary – except sometimes they don't. I was the same person I always was, just hidden under layers of social conditioning and other people's judgement.

People only judge out of fear or ignorance. They wouldn't dare do the things I did, so why should I care?

My desires had been hidden and my excitement dulled. Now I was running away, seeking it out.

There was another voice in my head which was more re-assuring and comforting, a familiar voice. It was a recent voice belonging to someone I barely knew but respected immensely. This person was an enigma, although on paper just an ordinary everyday person, but one that had caught my attention.

"You'll do this, you'll make it happen. You're a strong independent woman, you can do anything you put your mind to, I know you can."

The voice filled me with pride. Having lost most of my self-confidence by this point, these words made me feel warm inside. I was going to make everyone proud and in turn seek the freedom and excitement I was craving.

The voice made me love myself, it was kind and thoughtful but also realistic and down to earth. This person didn't know the effect they had on me; in fact, it was quite the opposite.

Then suddenly, as if to break my moment of self-love, *'ping!'* a message popped up;

31

'Enjoy your trip, you fat simpleton!'

This time, a message from a more familiar voice, one which in recent months had become a voice of hatred and jealousy. A voice that filled me with self-loathing and unworthiness.
The text hit me like a punch in the face. The words punctured my heart and with it, I could feel my self-esteem ebbing away once again. Crushed and angry I sent back;

'Merry Christmas to you, as well!'

I blocked that number for the tenth time in as many weeks.
These types of messages usually appeared at an opportune moment to ruin a happy thought. Like a black cloud on a sunny day. The stupid bastard knew my Achilles heel – knowing that a message about my weight would wound like a knife to the heart.
But this was my trip, my experience, and no one was going to stop me enjoying it.

I boarded the flight still angry and spitting blood from the comment. I needed reassurance so re-read my message from a happier voice:

'Hey Beaut, have the best time!'

I caved into the kindness and forgot my need to resist a reply and thus appear in control.

'Merry Christmas to you my wonderful friend!'

Chapter 6
The Wheels Are Coming Off

"Steve, what the fuck is up with you?" I screamed.

It felt like banging my head against an impenetrable concrete wall. He stared at the floor, sullen, like balloon that had all the air taken out of it. Saggy and sad; not daring to make eye contact with me.

"I don't love you anymore, I can't help it!"

He sobbed, holding his head in his hands with shame and allowing the tears to trickle down his cheek.
He was a broken man. He rarely cried, and here I saw all 6 foot 4 of my beautiful husband reduced to tears like a boy who'd lost his favourite pet. It was tragic to see him in this broken state – a man I'd spent the best part of thirteen years with, a man I loved with all my heart, and there he was curled up in a ball. I couldn't do anything to stop him.
As the words left his mouth and trailed in the air and I wanted to catch them and put them back.

My ears didn't want to hear it.
My mind tried to block out what he was saying.

As those words trailed across to me, they struck as a high-pitched tinnitus, rattling around my inner ear;

"I don't love you anymore".

With one small sentence my life was crushed and my future as I knew it had gone.

My thoughts turned to Sophia; how would she cope – how would we cope? What would happen to our lovely little family? A family that only days before this was normal.

I hadn't grown up in a divorced family as such, my parents split when I was twenty-eight and even though they were constantly at each other's throats, it had still hit me like a juggernaut.

It wrecked my maternal family and I hadn't spoken to my Mum since. I knew divorce was destructive and toxic.

How did this happen?

What have I missed?

Was there someone else?
Why would he say this?

I was firing the questions out to Steve like cannon balls hoping to hit a target.

"We were a team. 'Team Kaye'. The dream team - weren't we?"

I said to him with a fake smile, putting my arm around him before he uncoupled my arm and re-coiled in shame.

I attempted to reason with myself in my head. 'Yes, he could be a pedantic pain in the bum, and I rambled on a bit too much and spent far too much money. But we were solid, weren't we?'

It was about midnight and I was dazed. I felt punch drunk like a boxer after too many rounds in the ring. We talked for about an hour and he assured me no one else was involved.

I said we could try and make it work and fall back in love with each other again. I desperately wanted that more than anything in the world.

I needed my husband and I knew he needed me. I suggested marriage guidance or mediation. I was willing to try anything, but he said he

34

was emotionally dead. He was a corpse of a man lying there soulless and empty on the floor.

Had I done this to him? Had I beaten the life out of his personality, by demanding we move?

Things had definitely got a bit boring, but that was normal after getting married and having children. There's not much else to achieve and strive for once all the major life events have taken place. A few days in the sun and a trip away could solve that. I begged him to talk it out and make it work. I had friends who had regular stand up rows and fell out almost daily, this wasn't us. We had respect for each other, we loved each other really.

We could make it work, it needed to work, or I couldn't cope.

Still staggered by his confession I waited until he was asleep, and I got in the car and just drove. I drove and drove until I was down the motorway. I had no idea where I was going, I just needed to get away. As a small child I was always running away, never happy being in the same place for too long. On this night I was running home, to my real home – but where was that? It was a fictitious place I'd made up in my head where I was happy and free.
It was dark and the lights shining on the M6 almost blinded me. I turned the radio up to drown out the noises in my head. Heart FM was playing 'Love Yourself' by Justin Bieber. I should have taken that as a sign as I spent the next few hours driving round wondering why my husband didn't love me and what I would do without him.
I'd wanted to get out of the house and away from what had been my sanctuary, but I didn't know where I was going. I was driving to nowhere. My sanctuary had been destroyed by a tidal wave of rejection and I'd been thrust into loneliness. I went in search for somewhere that felt normal.
I got to Hilton Park services and I phoned my friend in Italy who never seemed to sleep. I knew she'd be a good ear.

35

"I don't know what to do Lucia, he says there's no one else. Why doesn't he love me? Am I so horrible and disgusting to look at that he can't love me anymore?'

"Don't you be silly you're beautiful outside and in. His mum's ill and she's never going to get better and surely that's got to affect the way he's behaving," she said trying to re-assure me.

She was right. His mum was deteriorating, and I'd put far too much pressure on him. Every conversation I'd had with him had been about dementia, almost to the point of tedium. Even I was starting hate hearing myself talk about it

"Let's be dementia friends," I'd said, in hope we'd have a shared knowledge and therefore something to talk about.
"I've written a poem about your Mum's dementia; do you want to hear it?" I'd excitedly revealed to him one day.
"Let's watch Still Alice, the book was brilliant, this disease fascinates me. Did know you when people have dementia..."

I'd said before being interrupted

"Fuck your interminable ramblings, don't you ever shut up, you thick bitch?" he raised his voice at me.
"Don't you ever stop fucking talking? Why can't you just sit in silence like normal people? You're doing my fucking head in! You latch onto an idea or new thing and that's it, it's a bloody obsession for you! Just shut the fuck up, your research is all bollocks and unfounded." he'd said a few weeks earlier, when I was just trying to help.

This wasn't like him. He'd always joked about my chatter before, but now his words were more pointed, nasty even.
As I drove through Birmingham, my addled brain was spewing out these conversations, re-living them in my head, making me feel sick with insanity.

36

When did we start these arguments?

For the first 10 years we hadn't had a crossed word. We had got along nicely as I worked away most of the week – arguing wouldn't have been beneficial. Now we seemed to be constantly at each other's throats.

I'd inferred that maybe he had someone new and was using his bitterness to push me into leaving him.

"Don't be ludicrous Elise, no one wants the pair of us, we are made for each other," he had joked in his usual glossy tone, which made me feel at ease.

He was right, I couldn't have thought of any two people more perfect for each other.

Now he resented me. What for? For constantly reminding him his Mum was ill? For actually caring about her? For actually giving a flying fuck about the woman? I loved that woman so why wouldn't I help? Lord knows she'd done enough for us, caring for Sophia while we worked away. I couldn't have managed in the early days without my lovely Mum-in-law.

I'd only had 12 weeks maternity leave and she'd been there for us to take over and help out.

The motorway lights and cat's eyes shone brightly with a sharp yellow glow that seemed to be boring a hole into my retina, stinging my eyes until they watered uncontrollably.

Road signs flew past me. Walsall, Wolverhampton, Wednesbury. Wednesbury had only been good for one thing; Ikea, other than that it was a pointless junction leading to nowhere exciting.

The M5 junction came up and I contemplated for a brief second driving to the south coast. I was getting further and further away from home and a long trip in this stressed state was probably not the safest option.

Sophia and Steve were both tucked up in bed. Sophia would never know, and Steve wouldn't care. Like last New Year's eve when he locked me out after a small argument, leaving me to walk around the village at 2am.

Something was starting to go wrong then.

Sophia and I had taken the first National Express bus up to Leeds to stay with Dad – my lovely Dad. Steve had spent the next 3 days calling my Dad fearing we would never return. He never apologised though, instead I did for being such a 'gobby' wife who wouldn't shut up, and I vowed to be quieter from then on.

I drove the 45-minute journey into Birmingham. I love a big place. It was the weekend, and the city felt alive with action. The streetlights were glowing, the bars were fairly busy and had a few people hanging around – although much quieter than the pre-Christmas period had been. I suppose most people were broke.

I wound down my window and let the cold air snap against my skin. It hit me like a blast of ice waking me up with a jolt. I suddenly felt a huge distinction to the snug warm car I'd been sat in for almost an hour.

I hadn't a clue what I was doing. I just wanted to feel alive – alive like the city.

But I felt dead, dead inside and completely numb.

My numbness was an empty void. I was stripped of my self-esteem and purpose. I started to wonder how I was going to tell Sophia that Mummy and Daddy aren't together anymore.

I felt that void spread throughout my entire body. My hands were numb, my body was numb, my jaw was clenched and numb. I jutted my jaw in frustration and anger whilst my teeth crunched back and forth. I felt like I was going to grind them to dust.

My lifeless limp body felt like I'd been injected with novocaine for a filling. I just couldn't feel a thing. My heart was the only thing I could feel. It felt heavy, like it had been replaced with a brick, weighing my tire body down.

'My husband doesn't love me' I told myself.

Why?

Am I too fat?

Getting too old at almost 40?

What is wrong with me that I can't keep my husband happy?

What will people think? Everyone would have a good laugh at my demise, less so Steve's.

'Look at the glory couple, not so smug now, are they?'

'Look at her letting herself go with a husband like that, how did she expect to keep him?'

'He was never going to stay with her, was he? She always thought she was better than us, with her flash car and big shot job.'

I was going to die of humiliation on that school run, while they all talked and gossiped about me. A group of vultures waiting to eat their tasty prey.
People were waiting for me to fall and they would finally get what they wanted. I wasn't a local, I wasn't one of them.

All these conversations I had with myself – I was losing my husband.

Why?

It wasn't going to happen; I was going to put up fight. I was going to make him love me again, and the school mums weren't going to get their juicy piece of gossip to chew on.

Chapter 7
The Flight To Dubai

The flight to Dubai was fairly standard and one I'd taken many times
before when I'd had my decent job and salary. I liked Emirates,
regardless of what class you fly in they always make you feel special.
However, this time there was no turning left and receiving my bubbly
in business class, sprawled out watching T.V. As I queued up with
everyone else, I looked longingly at the cream leather recliners and the
tray of champagne perched on the side.

I turned right and moved towards my seat at the back of the plane.
There was no snacks or arrival drinks, just a warm lemony towel to
freshen up.

Who did I think I was anyway? I'd been brought up in a mining
village north of Leeds. My family weren't flash, they weren't even
middle class. I was the Granddaughter of two hard working miners.
My Dad worked in a factory and Mum always worked in retail. We
weren't posh, we were simple – although Mum did think she was a bit
grander than the rest of us.

In way I was happy, it gave me the aspiration and willingness to smash
the norms.

I'd just worked hard to get to travel business class and in doing so,
elevated myself to pseudo middle class status. A status that only
existed in my head and was brought out to show off and fit in at work
and with other self-elevating types. It wasn't nice behaviour; I wasn't a
nice person. At least not on the surface. Underneath it I was lovely
and soft.

The Cancerian self-protective hard shell came out too often, and
recently that's all people had seen.

I sat comfortably in my seat and attempted to clear my unsettled
brain. Mid-way through the journey I had a plastic cup of warm
cabernet sauvignon which I downed in two gulps. I attempted to sleep
while cramped up in economy. I was too tired to watch a film so opted

for music, something easy listening, a meditation app to get me in the Nepali spirit.

I fell asleep for most of the journey, knowing that once I arrived in Dubai, I was well on my way to enlightenment. India then onto Nepal – the expectation pent up inside of me ready to explode and overflow. I didn't know if I should laugh or cry; or both. I was turning into an emotional wreck. My crying had taken on epic proportions, then getting angry at life, then crying some more.

Before Steve had left and all this had all started, I rarely cried or got overly emotional about things. But now I didn't know what was up with me. I cried too many tears in too many months and none of them were joyful tears. I yearned to cry joyful tears, to be taken out to dinner or even lunch, and to be told I was wonderful and a delight. I wanted to cry at the overwhelming nature of such words.

I come from an emotional family and crying was never deemed alien or strange. My whole family cry, even the men. Somehow being with Steve, I'd learnt to toughen up and managed to hold back emotions, particularly as my status in life was unimportant.

Looking back, I'm not sure it was a healthy thing to do as tears are a natural reaction. Too much emotional suppression could manifest in physical problems.

I knew so many men who couldn't express themselves for fear of looking foolish. So many men who had transactional relationships and bad marriages because they didn't want to show weakness.

I wanted to cry joyful tears and I to feel like myself once again – a dreamy happy-go-lucky little girl. I seemed to have developed multiple personalities; all of which conflicted and none of which were truly me. I joked to a friend that when I cleared my house out, it looked like someone with ten personalities lived there. I suppose you can't label me or put me in a box. Labels are for other people to use; it enables them to identify with the familiar. I hate labels and boxes.

I landed in Dubai at 6am on Boxing Day. Dubai airport is a hub airport and with many people using it as a transit to get to other places. It's like Euston station, only much cleaner.

41

No one has time in Dubai airport, everyone is just passing through. A half-way house to their final destination and Asian holiday, a Singapore business trip, or Australian holiday of a lifetime.

The last time I'd been there I was on business; I was married with a family back at home and had a good job. I'd shopped, eaten, and had a laugh with work colleagues. This time I was alone, with none of those things.

There were some subtle signs of Christmas around the airport; a winter wonderland and feeble attempt to cater for the ex-pat children going home to Europe, but it was nothing special. The giant plastic polar bear on the entrance looked worn and tatty and not in keeping with the glitz and glamour of Dubai.

It reminded me of a tired-out Blackpool illumination display, the first one I went to as an adult.

A display that I'd adored as a child but looking at it with an adult's eyes had a dwindling appeal.

I text my old boss having not spoken to her in months,

'Hi! Guess where I am?'

I took a photo of a gift shop selling plastic camels and T-shirts with I love Dubai written on them.

I loved our business trips to Dubai. We used to have such a laugh sharing a swanky apartment and eating in while working away. The apartment always overlooked the skyline of downtown Dubai.

She texted me back;

'Get me a present! And go and treat yourself to a massage!'

So, I did! I sat in the chair in the middle of the airport and closed my eyes while I was massaged, pummelled, and relaxed. The tension in my body from the last few months melted away and my mind drifted to better days ahead.

Chapter 8
Unravelling

Saturday night on Broad Street was busy bustling with people socialising. Couples coming out of restaurants arm in arm, snogging teenagers, friends hugging each other - there was love around me everywhere. Everyone seemed to be having a romantic time, even the drunks seemed happy as they staggered from bar to bar singing at the top of their voices.

In contrast, I felt empty and lonely.

I'd felt lonely for a long time at this point, but I didn't want to admit it. I'd craved a husband who supported me, who was proud, and wanted to tell the world I was his. A husband who told me he loved me, one that cared.

In recent months I was an annoyance, an embarrassment, and a shame. He rarely introduced me to people and talked down to me in public. I felt like a massive, ugly, old disgrace to him. I wasn't the sparky pretty woman he'd married anymore. I was sullen and washed out.

'Why do you look like you are always in his shadow?'
One school mum commented I as walked behind him, hanging on his every word. He spent his time schmoozing teachers and other parents, wowing them with his witty chat. I just stood there like an onlooker, like I didn't want to be there, like I wasn't interested in my daughter's education.

But I *was* interested! I didn't feel important or like I had a voice anymore.

I felt invisible to the world. Was this what all 40-year-old women felt like? I was sure that's what happened when you turned 40 because I'd read about it in magazine articles.

I was tired of keeping up the image, tired of striving to be wonder woman. A role that I clearly was out of my depth in. I wasn't good enough to maintain it. The wonder woman act worked temporarily but it was so exhausting to keep up.

One little boy commented to Sophia, *'Is this your Nanny?'*. I was mortified at the time but sought comfort in the fact some people in the area had given birth to kids while in their teens.

Steve was the successful one. He was the one people wanted to talk to. He had interesting things to say. He knew about politics, financial affairs, and sport.

Everyone loved him, everyone thought he was a star. That's what he'd told me, anyway, so I believed it. I was happy to be in his shadow. Why wouldn't I be? The guy was amazing.

After driving through Birmingham, I went home. During that hour and a half journey my mind was overthinking, the cogs were turning, and I was shaking. My body buzzed with adrenaline vibrating vigorously like someone had given me ten intravenous shots of espresso. I liked coffee, but too much made me ill. I felt buzzy and sick.

I arrived home and walked through the door. The air was still, negativity was hanging in the balance, and the atmosphere could be cut with a knife.

Steve was in bed and Sophia fast asleep in her room. I crept round the house like a cat. Slowly putting one foot in front of the other delicately, as not to disturb anyone. I gradually started to open drawers, tipping out their contents onto the floor, then building up into a frenzy as I couldn't find what I was looking for. I moved furniture, folding and unfolding clothes in the laundry basket, my pace getting faster and faster and more frantic with every move.

Then my overthinking, overactive imagination went **mental**.

I wanted to scream but my voice wouldn't let me. Out came a cracked squeal, hurting my throat.

My breathing slowed down and I went calm. I was emotionless and felt unhinged like something in my mind had twanged. The twang was like a taut guitar string being pulled tighter and tighter before finally snapping.

I didn't trust my own behaviour or actions anymore. If I'd been given a shotgun, I think I'd have gone on a mass shooting spree in very cold and calculated way. I would have been like Michael Douglas' character in 'Falling down'. Detached from reality.

I was deranged and my blood turned to ice. I had nothing to keep going for anymore.

Then I began searching his things, looking to unearth the truth.

I checked his phone first, then his diary from the last and current year. I looked through his Sat Nav, cross referencing postcodes with locations and notes in his diary. I even checked his receipts. This behaviour was so out of character for me. I'm cool and calm, a 'whatever will be will be' type of person, I'm the chilled out white collar hippy. But now, I was so enraged. I didn't even trust myself. My heart was racing, and my head was pulsating and building up into hurried activity.

I slowly opened the zip of the side pocket of his briefcase, half expecting to find a ton petrol receipts or some cough sweets. I'd never looked in his case before, I'd had no cause to be suspicious. So why should I look? What was I hoping to find rummaging through his battered old briefcase?

In there was one solidarity piece of paper. Nothing to be concerned about, just a receipt.

Something made me inspect it further and as I picked up the crumpled piece of paper and held it in my cold shaky hands for what seemed like forever. I stared at the familiar Selfridges brand on it. A

45

brand that would normally make me shake with excitement. My intuition told me it wasn't a receipt for him or me - I hadn't seen anything new around the house that could have been a gift from there. I knew deep down I wasn't in his mind when he made this purchase.

On closer inspection I could clearly see a what was on the receipt: a £129 pair of women's sunglasses.

Either my husband had started cross dressing (which was high unlikely, this was sensible suit wearing Steve) or he had another woman. A woman he thought was worthy enough of driving to Birmingham and buying a pair of sunglasses for.

What the hell? Was this really happening?

I woke him up with an almighty screech,

"Who the **fuck** did you buy these for? I hope for your fucking sake, they're for me, but as they were bought in November and it's now January and I haven't seen them yet, I'll take it they're for another fucking woman!' I howled uncontrollably, my language getting more and more coarse.

My blood was boiling. I felt my rage overflowing like a volcano. I had lost control. My words came spilling out like molten lava, hot and fiery, with every intention to blister and hurt.

"Elise, Sweetheart, you're being silly," he said smoothly. "I bought them for a customer, to say thank you for the years' worth of orders," he continued.

"I mean I can't let my best customer down by not buying a small gift for her, can I Darling?" he finished, drawing out the word darling.

"So why did you pay with your personal credit card? That's our family money," I said confused.

"Sweetheart, we don't have family money, you know that," he said drawling out the word Sweetheart, so he sounded like Sean Connery's James Bond.

"You have your wage and I have mine and I can spend my money on whoever I want," he said, completely calm.

He was right, we did everything 50/50. When we went out for a meal, we'd split the bill, the same with holidays and household things. I worked hard to earn a salary to keep up with this lifestyle.
He had paid with his personal credit card, not his company one as he usually would do. The sunglasses were bought in November as a Christmas present for a female customer whose name he wouldn't disclose. In fact, he became very evasive about the 'customer' in question. He usually gushed about his customers, telling me every fact about them so I knew I them almost as personally as he did.
I still felt suspicious. So, like some crazed Sherlock Holmes I checked his Facebook and LinkedIn, determined to get to the bottom of this mystery.
Something didn't seem right with his story. Why was he being so secretive about it?

"Were they for Donna? Or Sarah or Kirsty?" I shouted names at him in the hopes of getting a reaction that never came.

I stupidly believed his story; he'd never given me cause to think he was cheating, and like a dutiful wife I smiled and apologised for being ridiculous and jumping to conclusions. Once again, I'd been sucked in by the long words and charm and the thought he might leave me, which was the worst thing that could happen.

I was going to save this marriage, and nothing would stop me. Not even some sunglasses wearing tart!

Chapter 9
First Evening in Delhi

I landed in Delhi around 6pm having travelled for 24 hours. I'd flown via Dubai to save on costs and partly because I liked the airline.
There was no sign of Christmas at all. No tree, no winter wonderland, no carols or songs playing. Christianity was just one of the many religions practiced here and not a major one.

Delhi airport had been renovated in the 10 years since I'd last visited. It was spotlessly clean with a large fashionable looking duty-free. It could have easily been mistaken for an airport in Europe or the U.S. I was disappointed as I looked at its trendy glass fronted shops. Had the whole world been sucked in by commercialised rubbish? I came to get away from designer labels and to experience life, not be enticed by Giorgio Armani and Hugo Boss, which in normal circumstances would have been difficult.
It this what this trip was going to be like? One disappointing thing after another as I discovered the entire world was actually a slave to the propaganda of consumerism.

I headed outside to get a taxi and was struck by how cold Delhi was. I'd got changed in Dubai airport into a vest top, leggings, and flip-flops – which I now realised what not appropriate for the temperature. I started to shiver. I was dressed for the 30-degree heat of Dubai, not the 5-degree heat of a Delhi winter evening.
I was never any good at dressing for the weather. I liked clothes and I dressed well, just not always right for the occasion.
Steve would always have a go at my inability to wear weather appropriate clothes, particularly on holidays that didn't involve sunshine.

"Elise Kaye, you never know how to dress for the right occasion. Too scruffy for a corporate dinner and too posh for a walk in the park, it's

48

poor parenting, didn't your parents ever teach you how to dress?" he'd lecture.

He always blamed my upbringing. In truth, I'd had a more wholesome well-rounded upbringing than him. His Dad had been a serial philanderer and his mum had been left waiting around for him to come home from what he said was his 'night shift'.
Many years she'd wasted looking beautiful and waiting around for her man.
My parents hadn't split until I was an adult and there was always family around. His family were not like that at all. Looking back, I think his words were shrouded in jealousy.

But tonight, I wasn't calling him. I wasn't calling anyone. I was going to embrace the loneliness and use it to my advantage; I was on this adventure on my own.

My body was as tired as a seaside donkey after a summer season in Blackpool. I just wanted food and my bed. I mustered up a smile to take a selfie and posted it on Facebook. This was the start of my trip and I was already exhausted, fed up, and tearful.

Why do I arrange these things without thought?

What sort of a pillock goes away on their own at Christmas?

Why can't I grow up and be normal?

I had been normal; I'd been a Mother and Wife. I'd danced in kids club on Canary Island holidays, I'd been to Legoland, Alton Towers, and Thorpe Park, I'd chatted shit with mothers at the school gates. I had been the hummus and celery mother in M&S Cafe when Sophia was little before returning to work.
All that had been taken away and I was finding myself, the real me.
Being the conformist never really suited me. The suburban life was

dull. The people were boring and lacked adventure: it depressed me. I was surrounded by suburban robots and I wasn't one of them. I had more in common with 20 and 30 somethings, and my soul yearned for adventure.

I went to the hotel bar and I did what any self-deserving Brit would do on landing in any foreign land; I had a beer – well, several actually - followed by a curry and the worst night's sleep I've ever had.
It wasn't because of the curry, beer, or heat - it was freezing. I remember thinking, since when did India get so cold?
I was kept awake by the noise. Delhi is a hell hole of noise and pollution, and it never stops.
All night I heard *'Peep! Peep! Peep!'* from the cars and lorries and people shouting in Hindi in the street. Finally, just as I'd started to go off to sleep, I was woken up by the call to pray at the local mosque around 5am.
They say New York never sleeps but compared to Delhi it's like a sleepy Welsh village. I'd been to New York and it was subdued and organised in comparison.

I woke up at 7am and had some fruit, eggs, and a cup of coffee and headed to the train station on foot. I don't know what possessed me other than this strong burning desire to experience adventure and be thrust out of my comfort zone.
Delhi by day is busy, smelly, dusty, hot and downright mental. But absolutely awesome at the same time.
The putrid stench of curry mixed with car fumes and a hint of jasmine makes walking around an odoriferous and at times stomach-churning experience, but you become immune to it after a few minutes.
During the daytime you can't see past the end of your nose from the smog, dirt, and pollution billowing out from exhaust pipes. I could feel my lungs getting tight and heavy as I breathed in, my throat was stinging with the carbon laden air. All I could think of was black bogeys and getting a chest infection - how very glamorous!

50

I wasn't even sure the insurance I got free with my bank covered me for my Indian adventure.

It was my second time in India and what struck me on both occasions were the colours. Everything seemed so colourful. The green, red, yellow, and pink saris on the women doing their daily shop, the spices being sold in bowls on street corners, the green and cream coloured tuk tuks, the gold gilt glistening from top of the temples.

It was alien environment but at the same time, I felt at peace and at home. There was no ex-texting me, no daughter wanting my attention, no unrequited love.

I didn't have any commitments or obligations. I was free as a bird - a very tired and frightened bird, but still free from drama. I wasn't quite free of my thoughts though.

I won't lie and say it was a stress-free trip, but I took it in my stride. I was a scared female alone in Delhi, paranoid I was going to get kidnaped and raped. No one knew where I was staying, so it would be weeks before anyone found me.

As I mentioned before, my next of kin was a primary school child who still believed in Santa Claus, what was she going to do, send a 'kissy' emoji and GIF saying, *'Don't stress Momma'*?

My plan for the day was to head to Agra to see the Taj Mahal, something we didn't get to do on our last trip here. Steve had caught Delhi belly, so our plans had been thwarted by the monument having it's Friday clean.

I set out on the 15-minute walk to New Delhi station, dodging the cars, Tuk Tuks, and fruit sellers on route. Arriving at the train station, I saw what had to be the busiest most confusing place I've ever been in my life – not to mention dirty, smelly, and very unnerving.

There were signs for locals, signs for tourists, tickets for north India in one place, and tickets for south India in another.

I was instructed, as a tourist wanting to visit Agra, that I would need to head upstairs. Upstairs was a long corridor stretching over three buildings with doors leading off. It was cool along the corridor, whereas outside was hot and sticky. I followed two twenty something female tourists, thinking that they looked like backpackers and were sure to know the way. I was just someone's Mum with a wild sense of adventure and too much energy, what did I know?

"Where the hell are we going?" screeched one of the girls in her high pitched New Zealand accent. It was the blonde, who much to my disappointment sounded like she hadn't set foot in a busy Asian city before.

"Up here," said the red haired, more sensible friend.

"Oh my god!" the blonde screeched again turning up her perfect button nose and yelping in her antipodean twang.

They were both wearing walking clothes and had back packs on, they looked the part. They must have travelled a fair way so I couldn't understand her horror at the sights of Delhi train station.
We have a phrase in the U.K. *'All the gear, no idea!'*. I didn't have the heart to tell them it.

As I looked across the corridor, I saw what caused the blonde girl's reaction. The room was filled with beggars with missing limbs. I walked past a man with no legs who was sat in the corner of the corridor. As I walked by, he flung his arms out to me and pointed to his mouth. A mouth with only about 2 or 3 teeth. He looked starving, poor guy.
The blonde girl yelled again,

"Oh my fucking god, get me out of this hell hole".

Granted, it wasn't the most pleasant of sights, but the poor guy had a disability and some compassion was needed.

"I'm so sorry, I can't," I said to the man, suddenly becoming very British. I wanted to help him but aired on the side of caution in case others decided to follow and there was an influx of beggars. I was too tired and unsure of my surroundings to entertain such antics.

'How awful of me' I thought as I walked away trying not to look him in the eye. I was sad. Sad for that poor man who, without a benefits system and no limbs, was out on the street getting hungry and cold. Back home I was too tied up in my own problems to see the need of people, too selfish to notice.

Here I had this burning desire to help. I wanted to help them all, but in a city with a population of 18 million there was no chance. Besides, Delhi had a thriving middle class who weren't willing to fund such things. Surely that was the starting point? India is a country with such disparity.

I asked for the train to Agra and was given a ticket to wait in a queue. This system reminded me of the deli counter in Sainsbury's. While I was there, I met a lovely Italian couple and told them about my trip. They were heading to the Punjab region for a wedding. We exchanged Facebook details so they could follow my journey and I theirs. It was a fleeting visit, but we kept in touch.

Finally, it was my turn. My number had been called in a 'come on down the price is right' type way. I could just imagine my name 'Elise from Staffordshire, come on down your ticket has been called' being called in a loud game show type voice.

Only on this occasion, I was told I'd missed the fast train to Agra by 10 minutes and the next one was late that afternoon, leaving no time to go and see the sights. The next day I was heading to Nepal, so bang went my trip to see one of the seven wonders of the world.

Let down once again in my attempt to see the Taj Mahal, I decided to stay in Delhi and re-live the trip I'd taken with Steve 10 years before. A time before marriage, before Sophia, before wrinkles and weight gain. I was a young agile 29 year old the last time I came here – not sure I was half as brave though. One thing I knew for sure, I was not this messed up and mentally tortured this first time around.

The new brave me was teetering on proving to myself that I could do this without a man. Without Steve, without my Dad who was always there for me, without anyone. I was still seeking approval, what did it matter if those men didn't think I was brave? I did!

I could have quite easily hired a driver to take me around and do it the safe way but hell, this is me, and I didn't go away to do comfortable or safe. This way was far more fun, if not a bit dangerous.

I headed out of the station with my tail between my legs disappointed. Back on the mean streets of Delhi, there was traffic and crowds of people like I'd never seen. The population of Delhi is around 18 million people, and that's just the ones that have been included in a census. There isn't a square inch of space between you and the next person.

People strewn in the streets, cripples, children playing with string and the inner of an old football. It was like a scene from a war film.

Delhi was alive. Delhi was vibrant. But I was still half dead.

Half dead but gradually waking up.

Chapter 10
Making It Work

Seven agonising months had passed since I found the sunglasses receipt. I loved my husband and didn't believe for a second he would jeopardise our lovely life.

'Why would he give up what we'd worked thirteen years to build? He'd be ridiculous to do that!' I comforted myself with this thought. I know I was annoying at times, but I was okay, I was fairly easy to live with. Maybe a bit too independent and stubborn at times – I was well aware of my limitations and the fact I annoyed people and talked a bit too much. I never asked for help and would always pay my own way, but I did what I was told to by Steve most of the time.

I tried to put on a brave face for our daughter's sake, for my family. But something had gone.

His behaviour got worse and he became snippy and rude with me, constantly undermining me. I couldn't do anything right; I dressed too young for my age, my make-up was hideous, I couldn't load the dishwasher properly. He would take everything out and re-load it, saying I couldn't even do the simplest of tasks.

I couldn't clean or iron correctly. I should workout more, do my hair differently, outperform at work instead of being 'Miss Average'.

"The thing about you Elise is that you're forever going to be average," he said. "You don't have the financial discipline or self-care to succeed and you won't do routine, everyone does routine, but you think it's beneath you," he continued.

I didn't think routine was beneath me, I just didn't like it.

He even suggested I took ironing lessons from the women at our local ironing shop as I needed to improve my skills. Apparently, my poor upbringing meant I wasn't taught properly. In truth, I was exhausted.

I was sick of being super woman, sick of trying to please someone who couldn't decide if he loved me or not.

At my lowest points, I thought if I was better around the house maybe this could work. Maybe if I was a better housewife, it would keep him from straying. I refused to holiday in Thailand or Vegas or anywhere with prostitution for fear he'd go off with them. He liked a subservient woman.

I thought he might love me more if I was more of a traditional wife. I could cook, that was a start. Maybe women doing the chores and the family thing and men going to the pub was how it was meant to be. It wasn't me; it took away my energy and dampened my soul and the long term thought of this made me die inside.

It was the twenty-first century and I didn't want or aspire to be a housewife. I wanted to be an equal and wanted to bring my daughter up to think the same.

I tried so hard but everything I did was still wrong. I was miserable and depressed. I was losing my personality. I tried to be like some Stepford Wife type character, cooking and cleaning. I wore demurer make up and sensible clothes. I traded my skinny jeans and short skirts for longer skirts and less sexy wear. My underwear became practical and unsexy.

What was I becoming?

I was turning into a different person and was so far removed from the theatrical, carefree person I'd once been.

He would comment on how slim and pretty other women were, how much better they were at household things, how they would support their husbands. My friends and family were disgusted with his contempt of me.

I wasn't the infallible woman I was expected to be and couldn't live up to his expectations. With every comment or snipe my self-confidence was ebbing and draining away from me like a cut that wouldn't heal.

56

"Do I look beautiful?' 'Do you like my skirt, my lipstick, my hair?" I was seeking approval. I was almost 40 years into working in a well-respected job with my own financial independence, yet still seeking approval from a man.

My dad said he'd always shown total disrespect for me and always talked to me like I was a 10-year-old girl. He had noticed this very quickly into my marriage but didn't ever tell me as out of respect.

"Who spends the day after his wedding day sat on the beach chatting up the locals?" my Dad said. I'd spent the day after we got married in the pub with my Father-in-Law.

Steve had wanted space, wanted to be alone.

I didn't even realise it, couldn't see it. It crept in over time so much so that I thought it was normal. In the seven months after the incident with the sunglasses, it had just gotten worse. He'd stopped pretending to be civil to me. He was mentally abusing me and enjoying it.
The one person who should supporting and being your cheer leader hates you and thinks you're useless. I felt isolated and embarrassed.

I was no slouch and there were a million things I could do that others couldn't. I could act and sing, I could hold a relatively decent conversation in Italian much his disgust. He'd roll his eyes as I laughed and fumbled my way through Italian conversations with various friends and was applauded on my decent attempt.
His grandmother was Italian, and he couldn't muster a word in fear of looking a fool and not being perfect. I admired people who tried to have a go at another language, it showed open mindedness. He said I was closed-minded.
My outgoing personality had started to erode. I went quiet, fearful to speak in case of saying the wrong thing or having my speech corrected. I daren't even text or write, too scared my spelling or punctuation was wrong.

"You're a bit thick, really aren't you?" he'd say as he pushed his finger into my skull.

I took part in a theatrical production and Steve's contempt of me was becoming apparent. It didn't go unnoticed by my onstage husband who noted;

"Darling, I barely know you, but I can see he doesn't care about you, there's no love there". He said if it had been his wife on stage, he would have bought her flowers and told her how fabulous she was. *"You deserve better than that"* he said.

Did I?

Steve had lots of offers from women lately, and he decided to tell me. This public adoration of him was increasing year on year.

"Well they need to get out more or you should hang out in classier places. You're a big fish hanging out in a small pond, aren't you?"

What had I become? A jealous snippy wife, driven by mistrust? I hated my pointed remarks.
I was starting to believe I wasn't any good and that I was lucky to be married to him. I was getting old. He would tell me regularly that he wasn't ageing, and he just didn't have that type of skin, all the time subtly hinting I was ageing.
I was getting fatter and had less time to work out with his constant demands. I was working long hours, looking after our Daughter, trying to run a home, and look beautiful. I was too busy trying to satisfy my husband to exercise.
He was getting thinner and working out more. His running regime was relentless and left little time for me to do my own exercise and I was forever tired. Looking after Sophia, looking after his Mum, and working, working so hard. I think during that seven months we stayed

58

together I looked the worst I'd ever looked. I was paranoid and lonely, and felt disgusting. Mentally and physically disgusting.

Jealousy had overcome me and was crippling my life blood.

My paranoia was getting bad, I was constantly checking every mile he did in the car, every time he was home late.

I was worried.

Chapter 11
Trying Hard

It was my Granddad's 90th birthday celebration up in Scarborough, we had a lovely weekend with my family celebrating. Surprisingly, Steve wanted to attend that. He liked my grandad.

In the day we walked along the blustery promenade, getting swept up by the wind.

We chatted, kissed, and laughed, and Sophia was running around on the beach. We played stick in the mud and football. It was a lovely day followed by a fish and chip lunch in the Yorkshire air. We were giggling away and chatting about last year's trip to Mauritius. It felt like the old days, and that I was getting my husband back.

We reminisced about our first holiday with Sophia when she'd pooed all over her jelly shoes and we then called them 'smelly shoes'. We were poking innocent fun at Sophia who was not best pleased.

The bad mood seemed to be swept away and replaced with a loving family one. At last we were finally getting somewhere; this was really working out, and everything that had happened before was just a phase.

We ended our weekend in the pub having a lovely lunch. Sophia was colouring in a Frozen picture, I was drinking cider and touching my husband's leg. I was happy, a snapshot of bliss amongst the past few months of hurt. We'd recently made love, and it felt passionate and amazing, the most amazing I could remember in a long time.

Then his phone rang and up popped a name and number of an old school friend of his.

A female.

A woman for some unknown reason I had taken an instant aversion to on first meeting her some 10 years before.

This woman regularly looked down her nose at me and sneer in the local supermarket. She made me feel uneasy. She and Steve had been on a school reunion 2 years ago and I had a fleeting thought that he might be having an affair with her.

She was trouble, I could tell. I never liked her when others would tell how sweet and wonderful she was. I found her quietly sly and manipulative and I know she had been in my house for coffee as she left some sunglasses behind on one occasion. I couldn't put my finger on it, but I'd never liked her. She always seemed to be trying to get Steve's attention and walked around with an air of authority, although there was no substance to back it up.

I was a career woman, reasonably attractive, with a massive circle of friends. I dressed pretty cool and had hobbies. I wasn't domestic goddess, but I was a strong independent woman who could stand on her own two feet.

She was a cleaner with washed out blonde hair, cut in a layered style from the 90's, blue eyes. Her makeup was like an 80's test palette from boots pale blues, greens, blue eyeliner, bright pink cheeks, and candy coloured lipstick. She looked and dressed older than her 39 years, floral dresses being her style. She was a mousey and quiet unassuming character, not ugly but not particularly sexy.

He couldn't be seeing her, I thought. Of course not, I reasoned with myself. A woman like that would never keep Steve's interest. A woman like that couldn't keep up with his demands and his admirers.

Why was she calling? I hit the roof.

How dare she call my husband?

Where's her bloody husband?

What does he think?

"I'm going to call her fucking husband; he needs to know!" I bawled at him my voice getting shriller with every syllable.

"We're just friends Elise, stop getting jealous," he said calmly in his usual cool and charming voice.

Something didn't feel right, so I decided to push his buttons.

"I bet she's gutted BHS have gone bust, the granny dressing fraggle. I'm more of a Zara, Top- shop kind of a woman and she goes for an older frumpier look, doesn't she?"
I was clutching at straws hoping he thought I was far sexier and cooler than her.
I was nasty about her hair, her makeup, her job. All superficial rubbish which I now know revealed my own insecurities. I think Steve secretly got a kick out of it at the time as it exposed the self-loathing part of my personality. It also made him feel special that two women were fighting over him.
He constantly defended her which riled me more. I became incandescent with rage. My blood was boiling, and I screamed

"You're fucking that stupid skinny fraggle, aren't you?"

He slapped my face, leaving me in shock and saying I should start to shut my big gob and, lose some weight and be more useful round the house and that he shouldn't have to show me how to clean I should be showing him!!
I'm no feminist, but that was red rag to a bull.

I threw myself into work and lost weight, changed my hair, changed my lipstick from chocolate brown to pillar box red, all to keep my husband from being swayed by the fucking school cleaner.
Why was I so bothered? What was I thinking?
Meanwhile, and through all the turbulence, my boss left work and I was promoted. Largely due to the damn hard work and hours I'd put

62

in the few years prior. I was always worked hard and was very creative. I was good at my job and it defined me. In fact, most of my conversations had revolved around my job, what I did, and who I worked with. I was my career before anything - other than Sophia, and even she took a side-line at times, something I'm not proud of now.

So, with my head in bits, I tried to manage a team of 15 people and stop my marriage from crumbling further.

I wanted my husband back and was convinced she, the straw haired blonde fraggle, had taken him away.

I tried to be seducing and sexy to Steve. I wore new lingerie and nightwear, bought different perfume, facial treatments, even Botox. I cringe looking back at my feeble attempts at trying prove to myself that I still 'had it'.

I was invited to Benidorm to my friend's 40th birthday bash. I suppose this was the start of my midlife crisis. I got drunk and got chatted up by some very nice young men – my self-esteem seemed to return, just for a few days. I was never unfaithful to Steve, I just wanted to prove that men still found me attractive.

I was having a great time, but something wasn't right. I felt sick. The last night of the holiday I was so tired and sick I went back to the hotel. My friends called me a lightweight and weren't happy that I couldn't take the pace.

When I arrived home and for a few days after, I was still sick and tired. Really tired. I was snatching a sleep in the daytime between work calls.

Mine and Steve's relationship was at breaking point. I'd come back tanned and looking good with a new spring in my step and he didn't like it.

I was being sick. Was it stress?

Was it down to the alcohol I'd consumed in four days flat?

Was it something else?

Entering the chemist, I could feel my body gently vibrating with fear. I opted to go to the Boots in another town, just in case I bumped into someone I knew.
I quickly grabbed the package off the shelf and sheepishly crept to the counter to pay for it. I was a grown adult yet found myself sneaking around like a small child.
Back home, I held the packet in my hand pacing up and down the living room, moving ornaments as I went. The blue vase in the living room window was moved three times – the flowers arranged and re-arranged, impending doom welling up inside me.
Finally, I went upstairs to the bathroom, inhaled for 4 seconds, and then let out a big sigh, my body slowly relaxing as I exhaled.
I quickly opened the wrapper and took out a long thin white stick and removed the blue cap.

I sat on the toilet shaking. I was shaking uncontrollably as I peed onto the end of the white stick, getting some of it on my hand – I didn't care that the I had more pee on my hand than on the stick.
I started to reminisce about the last time I'd done this and how happy I'd been with my husband by my side. both eager in anticipation of the result.
This time I was alone. Waiting for the result and kidding myself I'd got an inflamed liver or stomach bug.

I waited for what seemed an eternity; weighing up all the possible outcomes.
If it was negative that meant me and Steve could work things out without the added complication of a baby. If it was positive, he'd have to stay with me and look after the child. We could be a little family unit; Me, Steve, Sophia and the new baby.
A minute went by and it started to develop.

Fuck.

It's pink.

I scrambled for the instructions just to make sure that pink meant positive. Not only was it positive but I'd picked a precise kind of testing kit, the one that tells you how many weeks.

10 weeks. I was 10 weeks pregnant.

Oh shit. I really wanted a baby. I wanted Steve, Sophia, and I to be a happy family once again. What was I going to do? Steve had been so distant. He didn't care anymore, stopped doing things around the house, and still insisted he didn't love me. This has got worse after I returned from my trip.
I toyed with the idea of keeping the baby. I'd already lost one baby prior to having Sophia and that had been agonising. I didn't want to lose another life. This was a baby, a defenceless poor child. I love kids, but I didn't want to bring a child into a loveless family environment. I was already struggling to make sense of it all and having a baby made things more complicated.
What I did next was the hardest decision I've ever made in my life but also the best decision for Sophia and I given the timing.

I couldn't get an appointment locally, so I drove 90 miles to have a first stage consultation in Doncaster. If I'd waited longer my mental health was sure to deteriorate.
They tested me for every STD going and they all came back clear. It was my husband's baby and I'd never been unfaithful, so I wasn't expecting anything else.

Steve dropped me off at the hospital and went off to play cricket like it was a normal day. He didn't kiss me or check to see if I was fine, didn't send a single text. He was angry with me for getting pregnant, it was all my fault we were in the position. He refused to speak to me and looked at me with distain.

It was confirmation that I was making the right choice, but it was a lonely, horrible disgraceful choice that I would have to live with for the rest of my life.

Inside the clinic I felt ancient, like some stupid middle-aged tart who'd had too many drinks and got herself up the duff. Many of the girls waiting in there could easily have been my daughter. How had I got to almost forty and ended up here?

This place was for foolish girls who made mistakes down to immaturity and peer pressure or those unfortunate to be carrying a baby, that wasn't going to make it.

What was my excuse? Stupidity, desperation, and trying to keep a husband who had already emotionally gone.

Not only was I unique by being the oldest. I was the only one on my own. Being on my own was something I was about to get used to. The other young girls were there with their mums, boyfriends, mates, grandmothers. I was there all by myself. By myself humiliated, embarrassed and so very guilty.

Looking back and seeing the series of events that followed, I can honestly say it was the best decision at the time for me. I wasn't some teenage girl who made a habit of this, I was almost forty on the verge of a marriage break-up and mentally ill.

My marriage was literally hanging on by a thread, so I did a brave thing and called his bluff in the hope he would declare his undying love for me.

"Steve, if you're not committing to the future why don't you just bloody leave!" I shouted at him.

He looked at me stone faced and dead like I was a stranger he'd never seen before. There was a silence between us, and Sophia was at school so didn't hear the conversations that followed.

I never expected him to, but secretly I wanted him to fight for me. But he didn't. I wanted to be re-assured that he adored me. I just wanted someone to adore me, I was begging for him to love me, but he didn't.

The silence lingered for minutes, my previous words about him leaving were hanging in the air.

"I've found somewhere to live Elise, I'm leaving you," he said without a tone.

Chapter 12
Second Day in Delhi

My head throbbed from drinking beer and red wine and my body was heavy from dehydration and sleep deprivation. I'd envisaged a nice first class train up to Agra followed by a stroll around the Taj Mahal. Although, experts tell me that is far from the reality of the place, so I was probably saved the disappointment.

It was hard remaining static in a place like Delhi, I needed my wits about me. I was determined to enjoy its wackiness. Delhi was kicking, and I'd decided I was going to kick with it!

People in Delhi will do anything for money. It's a chaotic bazaar of wonder, spirituality and sin – I loved every second. Not because it made me feel welcome or wowed me with its opulence and splendour; because it was dirty and seedy and scared the absolute shit out of me. I needed this, a jolt into the reality of others, people who were worse off. Away from the clinical dullness of the U.K and thrust on to the dirty streets of old Delhi.

Along the streets of old Delhi, I was accosted by men trying to sell me fruit, cigarettes, newspapers, guided tours, goats; you name it they had it to flog. I'm sure if I'd asked them to get me 20 grams of heroin and a one-legged prostitute they would have. Anything was possible here, but everything was so filthy in this part of town.

As I wandered around the spice market, the powder from spices combined with the grit from the pavement hovered around clinging to my clothes. My sandal wearing feet were grimy as I stepped through puddles of organic waste and my hair was thick with dirt. In a weird fetish type way, I quite enjoyed it. I likened it to having sex over and over again with a new lover, getting dirty just for the hell of it.

I enjoyed getting down and dirty, quite literally in Delhi. I put on a dab of red lipstick and I looked alright from a distance. I 'm sure I looked a mess and the smell wafting from me wasn't too pleasant in the twenty-three-degree Indian daytime sun.

Granted I could have gone up to New Delhi with its multiplex cinemas and high-rise skyscrapers. I could have eaten in Subway or Pizza Hut. I didn't want to; we had those things in the U.K. That wouldn't have been a fun or a life changing experience. I'm the girl who normally goes to Sainsburys in her stilettos, I wear stilettos and pajamas, but I hadn't gone on the trip to feel pampered or comfortable

I was determined to be scared so I could change my ways, stop pining for unavailable men and being depressed that life had dealt me the wrong cards.

I needed to be well and truly out of my comfort zone, and I was.

I dragged my tired body along the road to where the rickshaw riders were. For some unknown reason I chose the scrawniest, toothless looking driver I could find. *'Good luck mate cycling my fat arse around town'*, I thought, as I hopped on board.

The very lovely Akhtar (my rickshaw driver) and I went on an adventure up to the Red Fort. On our journey through the streets of old Delhi, we passed the temples, the guys on the street selling their wares, back through the spice market with its pungent smells of coriander, cumin, and organic waste.

The price for my 30 min journey was 100 rupees. I gave him 1000 (£10) and told him to enjoy it. That guy battled some real hair-raising incidents and almost got run over and hit by buses – and he had to cycle my fat carcass around for 30 minutes.

He'll probably take the week off now and get under his wife's feet, I told myself, I bet she's cursing me.

I could hear her in her Delhi lilt,

"Akhtar!! That stupid English woman, what is she thinking of giving you a week's wages for 30 minutes work? Now I have you here under my feet all week! Well, you better make yourself useful!"

I could just imagine him having to cook dinner and skin the chicken all under his bossy wife's beady eye.

I chuckled to myself imagining this conversation.

On my way up to the Red Fort, I had never felt so Western. I hadn't seen a white face in all the journey. One guy had even stopped the Rickshaw driver so he could touch my white skin, which was turning a nice shade of bronze.
Akbar said that the street people like to touch white skin in hope it brings luck, it wasn't sexual. Apparently the extremely poor Indians associate white skin with wealth.
I wasn't there to argue about anything like that, so I carried on letting him touch my arm. When he'd finished, we carried on with the journey. I felt used, like some weird prostitute who only specialises in arm touches.
Once I arrived at the Red Fort, I thought I'd entered some parallel universe. One where only white people and the occasional Indian were. It was like all the tourists from all over the world were sucked out of the Delhi airport and transported there without ever reaching the streets.
It may well have been that most western tourists had decided to take the less risky and less polluted option of hiring a driver. It may also have been that they had better hotels in smarter parts of town than me, so they never got to experience the true craziness – well more fool them I thought. My experience was fantastically dangerous and exhilarating.

I'd been to the Red Fort before and didn't have a clue what the place was or why it was in the centre of Delhi. I wasn't listening or didn't care the last time. I wanted to go shopping and get a tan and pose; I think we both did.
This time, not being a twenty something barbarian, I decided to find out more and take an interest in my surroundings.

70

The Red Fort is a fantastic terracotta pink building situated in the centre of Delhi on the right bank of the river Yamuna. It was initially known as the blessed fort (Qila-i-Mubarak) because of it was the residence of the royal family. It is now a world heritage site visited by many tourists.

Get me! I could practically be a tour guide. However, that sentence was taken from a guidebook, and this time I was listening to the tours myself. I spent a few hours there just wandering around in the warm December sun, without a care in the world.

After the Red Fort, I took a Tuk-Tuk to a Hindu temple, which turned out to be someone's private temple in their house, on a twenty-minute route along the main road. I was touched up again, this time by two transgender people, an odd experience. Two men dressed as women trying to seduce me. One either side of me, touching my legs and breasts while I held tightly onto the bottom of the Tuk-Tuk trying not to fall off onto the street below.

I have to admit, I was now feeling petrified. I was not only out of comfort zone, I was in another universe. I'm not sure any travel book in the world would give instructions on what to do in the event of being sexually molested by two transgender people.

As they both finished their bizarre sexual ritual, the cheeky people asked me for money.

I hadn't asked for a touch up in the first place. If I had, I would have preferred they wear something more masculine not spangly cheap looking dress. Dresses that were so short, I could see that they hadn't opted for the full appendage operation yet. Maybe they were hoping my fee would contribute.

I conjured up a conversation in my head, 'Sorry Mr Singh next time you touch me up can you wear a shirt and tie and not the short dress, it's a bit tarty for my tastes and I'm not sure the yellow suits your skin tone'.

I think they were the ones getting all the pleasure here. I was left feeling used and bewildered and expected to pay 30 Rupees for the experience.

71

During that ride I had more people stop to touch my skin, which was becoming less white, and a more lovely shade of orange thanks to fake tan and some sun. I bought a paper in Hindi – not sure when I was planning on learning Hindi – bought a bracelet, and nearly died a million times in the traffic, all without moving from the vehicle. And I thought my weekend in Benidorm was an eye-opener.

After my visit to the Temple house and a cup of Chai, I decided no more Rickshaws or Tuk-Tuks, I couldn't stand the trauma. So I walked 2.5km up to India Gate. A dusty, smoggy walk in which I was almost run over four or five times. Sweaty and filthy with blistered feet; I arrived at India Gate.

India Gate is best described as the Arc Di Triomphe on acid. It was busy and full of people selling things; postcards, light up wands, drinks, food. It was also full of tricksters, pick pockets, and fake tour guides. I stayed to watch an army parade then headed back to the hotel.

Being a Yorkshire girl, there is nothing we find more annoying than feeling like we are being ripped off. Delhi is a Yorkshireman's nightmare. I was expected to part with money and in Delhi, it's not only an expectation, it's the tourist way of life.

My day in Delhi in a nutshell
• Mental and weird
• Scary but exciting
• Where all the women? The city is male dominated.
• Bring on Nepal tomorrow I thought, I was more than ready for it.

Chapter 13
He Leaves

Steve left and went on to rent a house around the corner. He was a decent Dad so had regular contact with Sophia and even took her away for a few days to the south coast.

The hardest part about splitting up was only having my daughter part of the week. I hated it, and it took some adjustment. Being alone was crippling me, so I worked a lot as a distraction.

Sophia and I were still living in the family home and I'd see Steve regularly, so I felt like he was just working away. I missed him and I missed the family we had. Photos in the house were a constant reminder that we were once a family and we could be again.

I felt confident we could work this out and it was just a phase couples go through. We were a team; he'd always said that. When he came around, I always cried. He'd hug me, and just for a split second my troubles melted away.

I was starting to get caught up in the fairy-tale plot, his touch was warm and reassuring. I loved hugging him, his large stature made me feel secure. Then he gently whispered in my ear;

"This is nice, isn't it?"

"Yes, it's wonderful," I said dreamily.

Then, as if he'd suddenly been possessed by the devil, he sarcastically said through snarled teeth,

"If you hadn't got rid of that baby, we could have made it work, babe."

Like using the word *babe* made it more palatable.

This Jekyll and Hyde retort tore my heart apart. I could feel every sinew stretching and pulling, weighing me down as his words punctured the air with his snide tone.

I wanted another child but not under those circumstances. It's a tactic set to throw me off course and manipulate me. I mulled those thoughts around my head over and over but comforted myself in the fact that it wouldn't have been fair to the baby or Sophia. He knew this would damage me, he knew every word would pierce through my mind keeping me stuck in a state of guilt: and that's exactly why he did it.

Then, very slowly, I walked towards the fireplace. There hanging on the wall above was a beautiful family portrait. It had been taken at my friend's home in Sardinia the previous summer. I loved the colours in the picture, the yellow of the lemons on Sophia's dress, the green and pink pergola climbing up the wall, the blue of Steve's shirt. As usual I was wearing black, like some Victorian mourner looking out of place amongst the colourful backdrop of the Italian summer scene.

I gently lifted the family portrait off the wall and stared at it sobbing. Salty tears rolled down my cheeks, stinging my face.

I walked through to the kitchen and opened up the top drawer, took out the biggest knife I could find, and stabbed the picture. First in Steve's face, then in my face, leaving a smiley faced Sophia staring back at me. I didn't stab her face, seemed wrong. I couldn't stand the picture; it was a fake, based on lies deceit. A snapshot of a life that seemed perfect but never was.

I continued slicing it all the while adrenalin was building up and exciting me with every stab. For the finale, I cut it up into tiny pieces leaving the frame and numerous colourful pieces of canvas all over the floor. A picture left in tatters with torn remnants of a good time. That's how I felt about our family now. Steve wasn't willing to talk to me or go to marriage guidance counselling.

It was over.

My dreaded 40th birthday was looming and had finally arrived. I'd got used to the idea of spending it estranged from my husband. Even if deep down I craved his attention and secretly wanted him to rescue me and surprise me.

I booked for Sophia and me to go to Italy to see my friend. I wasn't staying in suburbia bored and lonely. Our flights were from Stansted and I hated every part of that journey, down to the airport. Steve would usually do the drive and moan about it, as I was the one who booked the flights.

On arrival I received a text from Steve saying to hang on going through security as he was working in Surrey and decided to come to the airport and see us off.

He turned up in his suit looking gorgeous and impeccable as usual and handed me a card. A large card, rather impractical I thought at the time, a grand gesture and more for me to carry – going on a Ryanair flight with limited baggage made it tricky enough.

I opened up the card and out fell a load of notes, £200 to be precise. I scurried on the floor to pick them up, Steve helping me. As we rose together, he looked in my eyes and sighed. My heart skipped a beat. Inside he'd written in it 'You'll never get old, you'll be forever young'. I cried when I read it and thought deep down, he must love me. I was convinced so much effort had gone into him turning up at the airport and the inscription in the card. I couldn't be wrong all is not lost, I thought, and my silly outbursts were making it difficult for him to come back.

We came home and I was still unhappy. I booked another flight. This time to Sorrento, a place I'd lived when I was twenty-one. I had an idea to visit an old boyfriend while I was there. I knew he was married now and had two children as I looked him up on Facebook. I also knew that he was fat and looked older than his forty-one years. I, however had lost some weight, and looked good for my age – if not a bit emotionally damaged.

Italy is like my second home and being in Sorrento and the Amalfi coast was just like returning to my youth. It was a place I hadn't appreciated the beauty of at twenty-one. More touristy than I remembered, and I guess I would have liked it to have been more touristy then.

Sophia made friends and played in the pool. We had a lovely time and met some wonderful people.

I don't know what I hoped to achieve by going to see my old Italian boyfriend. Maybe I was looking for nostalgic purposes, maybe I wanted him to leave his wife and tell me he loved me. Hardly, he was fat and old looking now and even though my self-esteem was in tatters I did have some standards.

So, off we went on the train to Castlemare then to Funivia, then on a cable car up to Monte Faito. It hadn't changed a bit. The little Austrian bar which bizarrely didn't look out of place in the middle of Campania was still there. Sophia moaned that the walk was too far, but we arrived at San Angelo hotel. It was just the same as in 1996 when I first arrived as a young woman, knowing nothing about Italy. I was a little bit nervous, my stomach turned over.

There was now a sandwich shop and deli over the road. Sophia was starving, as usual, so I ordered a parma ham panino and a can of lemon soda. Lemon Soda was a favourite of mine from the old days. As I ordered I tilted my sunglasses down and there he was behind the counter- Danilo!

He was fat and old but still had his charming smile. My Italian dream boat was more of a lumpy bowl of polenta nowadays.

I started to have a little heated chat with Sophia who doesn't like butter.

"Mummy, I hate butter it's disgusting, you know I hate butter,"

"Sophia I'm telling you, there won't be butter on there, the Italians don't put butter on bread, trust me sweetie, why don't you ever trust me!"

I took my sunglasses off and I heard a tentative,

"Ellii", spoken in a Neapolitan lilt.

I turned around.

"Yes?"

"Why you come now? Why so long? When I last see you?"

"20 years ago," I said giggling like 15yr old girl.

I tried to speak Italian, and he informed me my language skills were still terrible and I should stick to English – how cheeky!

He then introduced me to his lovely wife and two gorgeous children, and we spent the day there and had lunch. We chatted about his Mum, Brother, and the old days and about how his Father had died when I was there. His wife was lovely and spoke excellent English. I thought he was punching above his weight with her, and that was some of hell of a weight nowadays. She was lovely to me even knowing that we were once together albeit, not for very long, plus I'd had him in the glory days. She probably saw I didn't fancy him anymore.
He told Sophia,
"Your mummy spent two summers on this mountain with me". How romantic he made it sound. I suppose it had been for the innocent twenty-one-year-old me. The pre-motherhood, pre-married, pre-jaded me.

I was still wearing my wedding ring at that point, and as I left, he said,

"Bring your husband next time, I like to meet him".

I turned away and let out a tear and we set off. I will go back to that mountain one day; the view of Naples bay and Vesuvius is amazing, a non-touristy gem. Maybe with my husband, he'd love it.
The next day we headed into Naples ready to take the three-hour bus journey over to Bari to see Steve's aunt and cousins. I hadn't been to Bari since Steve's grandmother died some eight years previous and hadn't seen his grandmother's sisters since her funeral. The family had never met his Nan's namesake 'Sophia' so it was about time they did, I thought.
We arrived in Naples and I told Sophia that Mummy lived here when I was twenty-one. Naples is not renowned for it' glamour. I'd describe Napoli as an earthy industrial city full of gypsies, beggars, and toothless heroin addicts.

"Mummy, does grandad know you lived here?" Sophia said worriedly.

"Yes, darling of course he does," I replied.

"Well has he ever been?" she said.

"No, sweetheart," I replied.

"I'm not sure he'd be very happy," she said in her usual sensible tone.

"Well I'm still here sweetie and nothing bad happened," I said.

"You're such a rebel, Mummy," she smiled and hugged me tight.

Naples was a dive, not somewhere to bring a six-year-old. But I loved it! It was a slice of my youth and its gritty charm appealed to me, even it didn't appeal to my very sensible daughter.
I was the Edina to her Saffy, and we would muddle along wonderfully together. At times she shook her head in sensible disbelief at my crazy

78

antics. To her I was occasionally a 'cool Mom' but more often, I was a total embarrassment.

We arrived in Bari one hot sticky August afternoon. I was clinging onto the hope that Steve would think I was wonderful for introducing his daughter to his Italian family.
His cousin Paola picked us up. Paola is 7 years older than me, beautiful, and glamorous. I love Paola's sense of fun and I secretly wish I'd told her the story of our split. However, I was in denial and hadn't quite come to terms with it.

She'd had terrible relationship after terrible relationship and never got married or had kids. I think I'll contact her and go and stay at some point. She'd be a great friend for the future.
I pretended Steve was busy with work, so we were having a girl's holiday. Paola and Auntie Anna were besotted with Sophia. They loved her pretty face and her funny little character. My daughter is hilarious and kooky but sensitive and caring too.
We had a wonderful time with Steve's family. Auntie Anna said,

"You look like our family with your dark hair, you could be our blood,"

"She **is** our family," said Paola.

"Next time, you bring 'im and he must know Italian, 'is Italian is terrrrribil!" she said in her stern but homely Pugliese accent rolling the 'rs' as she spoke.

I let out another tear. I felt at home there. I loved the lifestyle, the sense of family. Ironically, Steve's immediate U.K. family were nothing like that. I cried so much on that holiday that Sophia said she was going to stop talking to me every time I cried. I joked we could have our very own swimming pool with all the tears I cried.

The poor child must have been so confused and hurt. I was too wrapped up in my own hurt to help her.

I returned from that holiday refreshed and felt like I'd done all my crying and got it out of my system. Steve came around, he held me and kissed me saying I looked good. I looked amazing and knew it. I'd started to wear more colourful clothes and embrace getting older, a privilege that some never get.

Sophia had been packed off for a weekend trip with Steve, Father and Daughter time.

I sat reading a magazine and my phone rang – my phone barely rings. My friends either WhatsApp or contact me on Facebook. It was my friend calling to ask if her and another friend could come round for a chat.

A chat? I thought this is odd.

I had that gut-wrenching feeling in my stomach that all was not right and agreed to have a chat without delay.

Just over a week after we returned from Italy my two girl friends came around armed with pizza and wine. One friend rarely visits due to living out of town and being loved up, so I was really worried.

Pizza and wine? This was not a good sign. It's a sign that we need to get pissed before a confession. Wine is a sign of bad news, but it could have been worse, it could have been gin. Gin is a sign of disaster or that one of them is on a diet.

It was nice to see them, and I was chatting away saying what a fab time we'd had with Steve's family and my old boyfriend.

"Steve came around earlier," I said happily "and I think we can really make it work. He kissed me, a really lovely long passionate kiss, he still loves me I know it".

I skipped through each sentence like a loved-up teenager in my own world. I failed to see the expressions on their faces.

"El, I need to tell you something," one friend said hesitantly.

"Go on, what is it? You're not pregnant, are you?" I knew she was desperate for another baby and was hoping this was the news. Her heavy wine consumption told me she wasn't pregnant.

Then she blurted out;

"I've seen Steve with another woman."

I was frozen to the spot. I gulped, staring into thin air. I started to tidy up items in the kitchen, moving the tea and coffee canisters, tidying crumbs from under the toaster, wiping work surfaces. I always do this avoidance ritual when I knew bad news was imminent.

"Was she a blonde?" I quietly muttered, in the hope that they couldn't hear me.

"Yes." my friend replied.

"Pass me my phone please," I demanded.

I rifled through Facebook and got to her page,

"Was it her?"

"Oh my god. Yes. How did you know?"

I suspected for a while, in fact years.
Back tracking, my friend had said they just looked like friends, they were looking at photos and laughing together. Like a mug, I convinced myself they were just friends, and continued throwing myself at my estranged husband, believing we were getting back together.

Still in the back of my mind I decided to drive past the house he was living in and there it was – her car.

He was seeing her, and this wasn't some fling. It had been going on for ages, possibly years. I knew it, he'd always gushed about how lovely she was and how gentle and great she was with kids. It made sense. All the things I was good at were no longer good enough. Suddenly being able to clean and babysit kids was the most important thing. This wasn't my husband. The man who'd gushed about having an independent woman in his wedding speech. I wanted to take a hammer to her car and smash it up. Something told me to be dignified, so I drove off and went home the bigger person. Being the bigger person was something I learnt to be over the coming months.

I was desperate to know the truth, but I wasn't getting any answers. I flipped my lid again after seeing her car for a third time outside his house. I demanded answers, but he shrugged it off and told me I was making him more depressed. She was his friend and he could talk to her.

I screamed,

"Name ten things! Ten fucking things that pathetic excuse for a woman can do that I can't. Name them!" silence from him. "Name them or I'll kick the shit out of you," I said, shouting every syllable of each word.

He was silent and a tear trickled down his face. I carried on,

"What is so special about her? Who the hell is this dim woman that stole my husband, because I'm seeing some plain Jane under achiever from the village who has nothing to offer! Seriously don't tell me you have gone off with her?"

"Would you prefer it, if it was another woman?" he said.

"I'd prefer it off you were shagging a man!" I howled back.

Now, I'm a bubbly, laid back person. But when I think I've been screwed over, I become like a character from a Tarantino film. Seeing I wasn't getting anywhere, I continued,

"Well she must be bloody amazing for you to leave someone as awesome as me," I sniggered nervously not actually believing at that point I was actually awesome.

Then he blurted out,

"Well she can mow a lawn."

A phrase that will be etched on my brain and was to become my mantra as I navigated my way through this tortuous journey of breakup and self-discovery.

"She can mow a fucking lawn, Hallelujah! Well let's get that woman a Nobel Prize, shall we?"

It also became my victory statement later whenever I achieved something.
'Look at me now! I can mow a lawn, aren't I fucking awesome?'

Chapter 14
Mrs Logan/Leaving Delhi

I'd started the day feeling tired and emotional, letting out a tear at breakfast due to lack of sleep. The hotel in their infinite wisdom had decided to upgrade my room to one with a balcony. Having a balcony means screechy, noisy traffic in Delhi. I hoped the lack of sleep was not going to be a re-occurring theme for this trip. I hated not sleeping. I can manage for days without food or warm clothing, but without sleep, I'm a horrible grumpy evil mess. Everything was irritating me and without sleep, I was a crazed psychopath

I was apprehensive about leaving the familiarity of Delhi and entering a whole new world. One, I hoped, would be more peaceful and zen. Somewhere I could forget about home and where I could calm my overcharged mind – which the lack of sleep had only managed to exasperate.

I had purposely done zero research on Nepal. My only facts about the country were the capital is Kathmandu, Everest is there, and it's nestled between India to the West and China to the East. I also knew they had a devastating earthquake there two years before.

My view of Nepal was a peace-loving country with lots of Yoga retreats, Buddhists, water trickling down hillsides, and softly spoken people like the Dali Lama. The land which provided musical inspiration for every spa I'd visited. My mind drifted off into a soft dewy daydream as I anticipated what was to come.

My daydream ended when I remembered I was still in Delhi airport. Two Italian women pushed in front of me at check-in barging past, causing me to drop my bag and my laptop came crashing out onto the floor.

My 'zen' moment was ruined and resulted in me shouting,

'*Que cazzo fai?*' in my stern 'Itglish' (Italian/English) lilt.
Which loosely translated meant, '*what the fuck are you doing*'.

I hate queue jumpers, it irritates me. It was something I learned to tolerate or even appreciate as I continued the tour.

I was delayed 3 hours for a 1 and a half hour flight and resisted my usual temptation to buy duty-free. This wasn't a booze cruise; I was here to help and be philanthropic and philanthropic I was bloody well going to be. I wasn't wasting money on buying rubbish.

The flight itself was drama free and relatively comfortable.

I remembered my neighbour, Mrs Logan. She was a 100 years old and always yearned to travel. I also remembered how ill Mrs Logan had been before I left and wondered if I'd get to see her again.

Mrs Logan was an ancient tiny figure of a woman who lived next door. Standing at only 4ft 10inches tall in her heels, she made me look practically gigantic.

She was petite and fragile in her physical appearance with a rather hunched back; largely due to osteoporosis and old age.

Her skin was translucent and paper thin and her arms often covered with purple bruises from randomly knocking herself as she got out of her chair to fetch her fags.

She was always smartly dressed, and if Mrs Logan had make-up on, then visitors were imminent. She often sat in her chair reminiscing about the past.

I'd never met her husband; he'd died a few years before Steve and I moved in next door, but I felt like I knew him so well.

We'd known her for over 10 years, and Mrs Logan had always been old. She was the little old woman from next door. My friends would ask if she was 'still going'. Mostly amazed at her lifespan given that she smoked about 50 cigarettes a day.

We'd never seen the beautiful young career woman she had been, the mother, the wife she once was. She was the little old lady who we loved dearly from next door.

This was no gentile old woman. What Mrs Logan lacked in height she made up for in grit and steely determination. She was a force to be reckoned with, and one of the most logically intelligent women I'd ever met. At almost 100 years old, she was sharp.

Witty, and amazingly on the ball. Nothing got past that woman.

I loved her. There were many who'd had a testy relationship with her over the years and subsequently fallen out with her, but not me. I respected and had learned so much from her. I didn't always agree with her views, mostly on things that showed the generation gap such as immigration or food tastes, but I was never disrespectful when hearing her opinion.

When I got married, I went around to see her in my wedding dress as she couldn't make the trip to Sardinia. I knew full well by the time I got home it would smell of fags. She was always bloody smoking, and low and behold anyone who questioned the health implications. She did drink gin in the early days of knowing her, but as time had ravaged her body, she'd lost the taste for it – but she never lost her appetite for nicotine.

Rather than saying 'you look beautiful, you look positively radiant' as I hoped she would. She would say,

"Don't you go wasting that brain of yours and settling down to have loads of babies now you've got married, will you? One or two should be more than sufficient I should think dear. In fact, stick to one. I had one and the childbirth was enough to put me off for life," she added as I squirmed. Half embarrassed, half feeling her agony.

"Oh yes, and you look lovely my dear. Very elegant." It was like an afterthought.

She wasn't one for excessive flattery but if something was nice or pretty, she would say so – if it still made logical sense. She had no time for flouncy language and unnecessary compliments.

She'd been secretary to the chief executive of the local mine and had been an elegant woman herself. There was still evidence of this as she sat in her chair with her best clothes and jewellery on.

She loved riddles, crosswords, quizzes, and sudoku. She had been an excellent pianist and could paint and draw fantastically well.

Her interests kept her mind active and young. She was very conscious of keeping her mind alert.

Her mind was young, but her body was very old and failing her more and more.

"*I looked in the mirror this morning, dear,*" she announced in her nicely spoken accent tinged with a hint of Birmingham. "I said to myself, who's that old bugger looking back at me? I didn't recognise her. When did I get so old my darling?

Don't get old, it's a terrible affliction," she sadly said to me.

Having lost her only child, a daughter, many years before, people in the village had told me she'd become a shadow of her former self.

To lose a daughter, husband, and brother within 10 months was devastating and something she never got over. I felt her pain even if I'd never experienced it for myself.

I was like the Granddaughter she never had. Steve was like a replacement Husband and Grandson depending on her mood. She'd flirt with him and always wait for a kiss. She eagerly waited for his visits so he could give her a big smacker.

Then when we had Sophia it made her day.,

"You've brought another little girl into my house and I shall be eternally grateful. What a joy, such a wonderful child.

Don't let her get fat! I don't like fat kids, I don't like fat anything my dear, it's a sign of poor health and poor housekeeping."

She had once called her cleaner fat and told her to eat less. The wartime generation didn't like excess, my Grandad was the same.

I admired the woman's honesty; you always knew where you stood and at her age who was going to argue.

She's always been Mrs Logan and she didn't divulge her real name to anyone. To her family she was Auntie.

I'm not sure anyone dared to call her by her first name. First names were disrespectful. The woman had lived through two world wars and numerous monarchs and prime ministers, so who was I to argue about modern-day naming rituals.

Mrs L had been part of our extended family over the years. I'd spend many a day just listening to her stories before Sophia arrived. After, it was shorter more frequent visits while Steve was at work.

Then Steve left us and I was too embarrassed to tell her.

Late September about 8 weeks after Steve had gone, I received a phone call.

"Hello Mrs Logan, everything ok?" I said.

"You tell me!" She replied in a stern way. "You better get around here and come and see me, because I've heard a rumour and I'm not happy."

"Yes, I will," I obediently said and put on my coat to go next door.

I walked through her rickety old wooden door and into her lounge which resembled something from the 1950s. Before I could take my coat off and put the kettle on, she blurted,

"And where does he think he's buggering off to, leaving his family? Well, quite honestly I'm disgusted!"

I was shaking and felt like I'd done something wrong.
"It's just temporary until he sorts his head out," I said quietly.

"Well I lived through the Second World War with a husband away and baby to look after, he can't just bugger off because he can't handle it! I couldn't handle it at times, but I did it and I'm here today to tell the tale.

He's got another woman I'm telling you. If I find out he has and he's left a beautiful wife and daughter behind, he will get my size 5's up his arse."

I let out a giggle and she shot me a look.

"Tell him he needn't come around here with his smarmy kisses and bloody flowers because I'm not falling for it! He needs a massive boot up his arse and told to come home. What do his family think?"

"Nothing, they don't care," I said.

They didn't care. They were so dysfunctional that it was nothing to them. So, I never really bothered to ask them.

"Well, I bet your dad has something to say!"

"He doesn't know," I said coyly.

"Well you better tell him, or I will!"

"*Ok,*" I replied not giving her eye contact in a hope she'd stop talking about it.

I started to cry.

"You can stop your crying; you need to be strong and crying is showing your weakness. I lost 3 members of my family in a year and I didn't cry once."
I hugged her knowing she wasn't entirely telling the truth. I'd seen her cry when she talked about her Daughter. Tears had trickled down her cheeks as she'd described her daughter as a child, at college, and as a woman.
She was a big softie really and even if she didn't let everyone see, I knew she was.

She was angry and sad for me and Sophia. I was touched by her protest even if it was a bit misguided.

Another time I popped round I shared my up and coming trip with Mrs L.

"How are you doing? Have you found yourself a lovely young man yet?"

"I'm good, and no I haven't" I replied. Thinking to myself, I have found a young man but he's certainly not mine.

"I'm going to Nepal Mrs L, I'm going to work in an orphanage at Christmas!" I exclaimed proudly like a 5-year-old presenting their first piece of school work.

"Bloody good for you, you will have such an adventure, I wish I'd travelled you know. I really envy you," She confessed.

"I want to hear all about it dear, the children's little faces, the scenery, everything, and don't forget photos, I want proper photos mind, no showing me it on your phone with my cataract. I can't see them. I really dislike those things, they make my eyes hurt," she said breaking out into some prose about modern technology and how you couldn't feel or touch things anymore and how life was better with Polaroid.

"Yes, I'll even do you a photo album," I said. I'd done one for Steve's Mum and all the family after her diagnosis, so she wouldn't forget them.

Mrs L was like my Midlands Nan. I did once tell her I loved her, and she smiled because despite her opinionated rants and old-fashioned views, she loved me too.
I left the house feeling secure and that lifted my mood for the day.

About a week before I set off, I received a call from Mrs L's family. I rushed round to the house with Sophia. I had to see her. When we arrived, the carers were there in the living room.

"I wouldn't let Sophia go in there Love, she ain't good," said one carer in black country twang.

"Well I don't care what you think," I said bossily. "Sophia and I are going in, she's like our Nan."

I snapped and barged past them holding Sophia's hand.
I was sick of people telling me what to do, and I was sad.

Mrs L was so small and hunched in the bed, like a child, fast asleep. We sat by her bedside and my brave, beautiful Sophia held Mrs Logan's tiny hand and cried. Sophia sobbed and sobbed.

"Mummy will Mrs Logan die?" she asked looking for hope.

"Yes Sweetie, I'm afraid she probably will," I said holding back my tears.
"But she saw her 100th birthday and not many people do that," I said, aiming to console her.

I turned to Mrs Logan and kissed her hand.
"You've had a good innings old girl, it's time to go," I said holding back my tears once more.

Then I couldn't any longer, they all came flooding out like a tidal wave through a burst dam.

"I'm going to make you so proud of me," I wept, knowing it would probably be the last time I saw her.

Chapter 15
The Singletons

With Steve gone, one of the first things I had to get my head around was being single.

Being single at forty was different to being single in my twenties. For a start, everyone seemed to be in a couple. Not being in a couple meant not being invited to things, things that involve being in a partnership. Dinners, weekend breaks, weddings - I was excluded. I'd suddenly become a social leper.

Single at forty also meant I became a potential husband predator, and therefore a repellent to friends with stable marriages. They were potential partners to steal or worst still, a target for bored married men looking to spice up their love life without their wife's knowledge – and weirdly on some occasions with their permission.

I wasn't a prude but even I baulked at the thought of someone's wife watching or joining in.

A simple put down was enough to deter the marrieds. Believe me, after what I'd been through, stealing someone's husband was the last thing on my mind; and none of my friends had husband's worth stealing anyway.

I was also a target for the other side, a team I've never considered batting for before becoming single. I seemed collect an army of lesbian admirers who thought they could sway the scorned man hater to the other side. I had endless jokes and innuendos with the girls at my sports club over this and secretly enjoyed the attention.

Unfortunately for them, I was a tricky case and I couldn't be swayed. Lovely girls, but not really my thing.

The truth is, I wasn't a man hater. I wasn't sure I even hated the ex. I think some men have a predisposition to cheat. *'There are some good ones out there who are happy with their lot, not all men are bad'* I told myself as I endeavoured to move on.

The other weird thing about being single is the freedom. Freedom sounds amazing to any stressed out busy working mum with a couple of kids and husband to keep happy.

But when freedom is thrust upon you and you don't have a choice, it's quite unnerving. I hated freedom. It had the opposite effect on me. It trapped me.

I couldn't cope. I'd spent a long time seeking approval and as a default would constantly consult Steve on my plans: for the week's activities, for holidays, choice of decor, what outfit I should wear to go out in, even which house I should buy.

Something as a control freak, he revelled in and often made suggestions. I even chose the Wi-Fi provider based on his request.

Why?

Why would anyone do this?

Why was I still letting him control me?

I was like a robot pre-programmed to ask permission. A robot who'd had 13 years of marital conditioning and couldn't escape this mindset.

It took a lot of hard work to break from past habits, enjoy my freedom, and to stop seeking approval. I didn't know I'd been controlled until I stopped being controlled.

Freedom made me scared. I could do what I wanted when I wanted, but who would know? What if I got into trouble? Who would care?

I remember having to write an application form for the Doctor and needed to put my next of kin. Once again, I cried – I always seemed to be blinking crying. I no longer had a next of kin. There was Dad – Dad was always there but I wasn't twelve and I was living over a hundred miles away. He couldn't get to me quickly in an emergency.

The alternative was a primary school kid and as she couldn't drive, I'd probably be waiting eleven years for her to come and rescue me.
So, I left it blank.

This freedom thing wasn't all it was cracked up to be; it made me lonely. It made being an extrovert difficult to enjoy. I hated being single and free when everyone else was in a relationship.
I did start to enjoy my newfound freedom but made many mistakes as I clumsily navigated my way through this weird unfamiliar territory. I wasn't good at being single, single people were cool and together, they were independent, and I didn't think I was.

I tried to continue with my life – which at this point seemed to be in tatters I started boot camp – looking back it was the best thing I'd ever done. I got fit, I could bench press, flip a tractor tyre, and hang off bars by my legs. A sit up would have wrecked me when I started, but I eventually got strong. My body was strong, but my mind felt weak. I met lots of friends and it became part of my regular routine. Boot camp was run by a guy who can best be described as everyone's naughty little brother. He was funny, crude, and farted a lot, largely down to his vegetarian diet and excessive plant-based protein intake. We had such a laugh great friendships were formed. Without those boot camp buddies I don't know how I'd have got through the months of hell. I'd like to think I was a ray of sunshine for them too, as we attended gigs, theatre productions and even holidayed together. Never have I laughed as much as with those guys. Most of them were 10 years older and I took their sage and sometimes weird advice as comfort as I went through my ordeal.

I was starting a new life but was still unsure of the relationship status of my husband. I knew he was lying to me but somehow, I still wanted to believe him. I wasn't ready to let him go, and he knew that. Those joining boot camp seemed to be getting divorced or on the verge of divorce. I wasn't sure if people turn to this sadistic form of exercise in moments of crisis, but it suited me. Lots of likeminded,

94

single people who had all gone through the relationship ringer. Some formed new romantic relationships: not me. I wasn't ready and was too bloody fussy. They were lovely people, but the single guys weren't exactly George Clooney.

I was a mess, not a physical mess. I was in great shape, but my head was shot.

It was the boot campers who introduced me to online dating – a concept I'd assumed was for social misfits. Back in 2000 when it was first introduced, I remember it being popular with the guys in I.T. The guys who couldn't communicate properly with the outside world, the geeks.

In reality, I'd already summed it up well – they were sites full of social misfits and geeks. Although the social misfits were sex craved players, looking for a one-night hit.

For anyone who has never experienced the wonderful world of online dating, here's what it's like;

An app-based beauty parade for tarts, saddos, weirdos, or worst still criminals. You are basically armed with the profiles and pictures of 100's of men (or women, should that be your thing). It was 10's in my case as my criteria was too strict. If you choose each other, then you can communicate. Some dating sites let you message a person you might potentially like. I found this all a bit creepy but was assured if I wanted to meet someone I'd need to persist.

"No one talks in bars nowadays Elise," a friend of mine informed me. "They're all too busy swiping left or right."

'What a terrible situation dating had become', I thought in my then very prudish approach to dating.

So, I cast away the prude inside me and decided to give it a whirl, what was there to lose? My dignity for a start.

It's surprising how when you're married you can go months without sex. Suddenly you become single and turn into a potential street worker.

So, channelling my inner Dita von Teese, I posed for and uploaded 3 photos of myself, all from various angles.

I hadn't taken a selfie since having Sophia, I was too vain and too insecure to let anyone take many photographs of me, and definitely never a full length one. I thought I was dumpy and bloated.

Steve had called me dumpy and stumpy when I couldn't reach the tins he'd put at the back of a high cupboard. He would purposely unload the shopping and put food at the back of the highest cupboard so that I would have to ask for help.

Steve always made me feel inferior in the looks department, so I hid away from the camera.

I wasn't particularly photogenic, as he'd once pointed out, so there wasn't any point.

"You take a terrible picture Elise, you should learn to pose properly and off to the side, you won't look half as dumpy then," he'd say.

Steve had done some modelling and since he left was doing more. I didn't like him modelling, I'm not sure why, but it made me uncomfortable.

My first few online conversations were great, and I was flattered by the attention. I was desperate to find a new love and on here I seemed to be getting closer.

I could also hide behind my keyboard and with the security of Tinder to conceal my full identity.

Men were weird – they put photos of their abs, beach photos, photos with their dogs, sporting events, skiing, running cycling, and oddly their wedding pictures. I was told women had photos with uglier friends, professional headshots, snapchat filtered, classy tit pics, and girl's night out.

So, this new style dating game was all about pretending to be someone you're not. A bit like Facebook for shaggers. All part of the game of deceit in this modern world to snare a lover and believe the bullshit and the lies that were told.

The next step after 'talking' on the app was to exchange numbers and this is when it went to all new level. In came the nude pics, dick pics, video clips downloaded from porn sites in pretence they had a huge film star appendage to reveal.

Wasn't anyone 'normal' anymore? Everyone seemed obsessed with image and sex.

Steve had been relatively conceited, but this was a whole new level.

Male genitalia is not my favourite image so why the hell did several guys wish to send me such rubbish?

I didn't know how to block people before online dating, but I blocked more people on my phone than I'd ever done in my life. Only for them to turn up as 'people you may know' suggestions on Facebook. I just wanted to go out and have a drink or nice meal with someone real; have a chat with a person of mild intelligence and sense of humour.

My first Tinder dating experience, or shall I call it a near miss, came within days of joining up.

I was messaging a lovely guy who was from Yorkshire and like me had moved to the Midlands. He was bright, seemed friendly, and was genuinely interested in me. On his profile picture he was tanned, muscly, and blonde. He was an artist which appealed to my creative side, a perfect match I thought. We had some joint connections in common via Facebook so it couldn't be all that bad.

It all seemed a bit too good to be true, but I went along with the fantasy as I was swept up in the whole adoration. He wasn't vulgar or crude and he seemed to be a nice guy.

We arranged to meet in a bar in Solihull but before we did, being an inquisitive type, I wanted to know more about him.

I asked lots of questions;

"Where in Yorkshire are you from?"

"Barnsley," he replied.

"What are you doing in the Midlands?" I wrote.

"I'm on an art course, I'm an artist," Interesting I thought.

He'll be penniless but creative. That figures why he couldn't meet me until he'd been paid Friday.

"Maybe I should try and be creative again," I said.

"You should, what creative things would you do?" he asked mildly interested.

This was sounding like a great prospect; attractive, mildly interested, intelligent, and creative.
We messaged more, then I asked if he was at the university. He said no, and explained he was at college in Birmingham. I continued with my curiosity which was by now bordering on interrogation.

"Why college in Birmingham? There are art colleges in Yorkshire. Why would you put yourself in that much debt for a BTEC in Art or whatever?"
I didn't hear from him for hours, something that isn't unusual in online dating. Had he ghosted me?

Then my phone went off, it was him. I was out with friends, so I dived in the car to speak to him.

"Hiya Love," he droned in his Barnsley twang, dragging out the words. His speech was slower than I'd imagined.
"I thought you seemed like a nice woman so deserved an explanation," he continued.

"Go on then," I said, rolling my eyes at the phone and waiting for him to tell he was married with 5 kids or something.

"You see love, I'm at art college," he drawled further, missing out vital syllables (as we all do in Yorkshire).
"Because… because…" he continued to drone and slur getting me a tad irritated.
"Well it's part of my rehab programme," he continued.

I gasped,

"Hang on wait a minute, you're a drug addict," I inquired and sank in my chair thinking I'd been sold a lie.

"Well Love, I used to be a drug addict and I'm on rehab programme in Birmingham, I'm a recovering heroin addict," he answered, almost proud about the recovering bit.
However, by his speech I wasn't entirely sure he had 'recovered'.

'What the actual fuck!' I thought in my head.

My very British response was;

"Well I'm so very sorry Sweetheart, but I can't meet you, it's not my world. I have a daughter, and I couldn't introduce her to this type of thing."

I put the phone down and thought for a couple of seconds.
Thank God he never knew my full name or where I lived, lesson learned.

Then the caring sharing me kicked in and I phoned back to say,
"Hi, I'm happy to mentor you from a distance – you are clearly a talented artist and need this channelling and it might help you out of your habit, if you had something to focus on."

I genuinely believed he wanted to get out of his situation and thought if he had the right support it would help.

I continued to message him for a couple of weeks, and he sent artwork for me to review. I even tried to find him a mentor.

Then one Saturday morning I was on my way to Yorkshire with my friend and took a photo of the Barnsley sign and messaged,

"I'm near your home."

He sent a message back telling me what a bad day he'd had the day before and that he'd lost his Employment Support Allowance, he had no money for food or to get to college.

I'm no mug. I'm well aware of a drug addicts, their habits, and lies they tell. With one click I blocked him and never heard from him again. I've seen recent photos of him on social media- the real gaunt looking drug addicted guy around various sites obviously looking for his next victim to rip off. I think had a lucky escape.

My mates have been on online dating some for years. They get players, con artists, and messers on their dates and on my first attempt, what do I get?

A bloody heroin addict – well done Elise!

My hairdresser thought this was hilarious and regularly re-lived this tale with his 'customers– ' or as he says,

"Clients Elise! We are not a sandwich shop; we don't have customers."

He loved my online dating tales, like he was vicariously living my new love life and relaying the stories to anyone who would listen. He loved the stories; they were interesting conversation fodder for his clients. He often embellished the tales for extra dramatic effect.

Not deterred by my experience I continued; I had a few lovely dates with a French guy who was vertically challenged and wanted to cook with me, a very tall 23 year old Iranian model who loved himself and kept telling me he was doing me a favour by dating an old girl. He went on to describe me as a dirty looking Catherine Zeta Jones – which was relatively flattering, if not a bit seedy – then ended up throwing me against my car in an attempt to lay me. Then another guy who was cute and pleasant, but shorter than his profile picture. What was wrong with these dates? Why didn't they match their profile? There was a lot of short arse men out there. At 5ft 4 inches tall I could hardly talk, but a woman needs to feel secure, and going out with guys an inch or two taller wasn't doing it for me.

I told myself this online dating was not for me. So, I came off the websites and concentrated on meeting people normally.

"You need to go on a classier site, one you have to pay for," said a friend of mine. "You'll get a classier chap on there."

"Really? I'm not paying to find a man. I'm not degrading myself. I know I'm 40 but God, has it really come to this?"

I couldn't imagine having to pay to find a chap. I'd been relatively attractive in my 20's and never struggled to find 'love'. Now in my 40's - really? Is this where my life was heading?

Occasionally I'd get out an old photograph, to see what I used to look like in the days before childbirth and a marriage break-up.

Taking the advice and largely due to lack of interest in real life, I signed up for a paying dating website and my friend was right. They were a better class, better jobs, more refined. No more wading through dick pics and having to decipher poor spellings amongst the poorly educated masses.

I dated an Engineer and a Barrister. What my friend failed to say that these guys were paying for 'dates' because whilst they were more refined and had better prospects, they weren't so attractive, and they were downright fucking boring.

I have standards and I just didn't fancy any of them. This is dreadfully shallow, but I did at least have to fancy them. Not only were they not aesthetically pleasing on the eye, but they were dull too. I didn't do dull; I did excitement and fun. These guys worked too much and spent days off chilling and watching T.V.

There were many dates with men, many times I bared my soul to these guys only never to see them again or be told I'm weird or crazy. I enjoyed the initial online dating buzz. It gave me a creative outlet for my writing. I didn't enjoy the smut or even meeting them, but I liked using all my witty lines on men on text messages.

Throughout this time Steve continued to message and annoy me, sending lengthy texts about the old days.

I kept falling for it. I just couldn't get past the charm and the nostalgia.

I couldn't move on and nor could he. We destined to be together forever. I was sure.

Then on the 1st January after a few months of separation months and long after he originally told me, he didn't love me; he announced that he was no longer friends with the school cleaner and they were going to 'make a go of it'. All my suspicions were confirmed in one text. They must have made a bloody good 'go at it' because within a couple of weeks he announced she was pregnant, and my world fell apart for the thousandth time.

I'd hoped until this point we would get back together, but a baby not only made that impossible. It also meant I would be linked to her for life, linked to the woman who stole my husband as she would be the mother of my daughter's half-sister.

Work at this time was becoming stressful, taking on a promotion when all this was going on was at best naive, at worst, bloody stupid. I couldn't cope getting out of bed, let alone managing a team of 15 people. There were days when I couldn't stand it, when I considered ending it all. Work was depressing and unfulfilling, I was flying to

Germany on half of the energy I'd had before. I couldn't be creative or think differently about things.

My colleagues were competitive and cutthroat, not because they were bad people, but because they were climbing the slippery pole to success.
There was jealousy and manipulation going on. It hadn't gone unnoticed by me, but I was just too tired to confront it. Travelling to Europe once a week was becoming a bind, I hated it. I hated everything.

It also made me question after seventeen years of doing the same thing whether I was in the right profession.
So, I took time off sick. I was sick, very ill, and burnt out. I'd spent the entire time with Steve trying to keep up, to the prove I was someone. My days had been filled with trying to prove I could do everything, for Steve to be proud of me and tell the world.
I'd spent years in a constant flux of working hard, earning money, spending money, holidays. Then I crashed, I crashed and burned, and I became a shadow of my true self.

I was depressed, and it was only made worse by lonely nights when Sophia was with her dad.

I wanted to re-build my life but didn't know where to start. I'd hit a brick wall of despair and I was drinking, heavily drinking. I had defined myself by my job, I achieved what I set out to do, I was driven. Then I'd suddenly lost my will. I needed the money because I'd got used to the lifestyle.
Meeting new people was difficult. They'd ask what I did – why are people defined by their jobs?

I was off sick that was it. I was empty and lonely.

A spark was missing, something wasn't fulfilling me. Being with someone for thirteen years meant I lost my identity, what made me, me.

I couldn't tell you what I liked or disliked anymore, because I only liked and disliked what my husband had.

I spent my life managing my husband's expectations of me. I was the Mother, the Wife, the businesswoman, the competitor, the actor, the cook, the linguist, the sportsperson. I was whatever I thought he wanted me to be. But one thing I wasn't - was me. I couldn't tell you where Steve started and I ended because I'd been moulded so much by him, that I actually didn't know.

Someone had once joked at work saying, *'I bet you wear the trousers at home!'*. The truth was I didn't. I was strong, but Steve always got his own way and I let him for an easy life. If he didn't get his own way, I feared he would leave me.

There was no purpose to life other than going to work and looking after Sophia, which don't get me wrong is lovely, but she's so independent she doesn't take a lot to look after. The school run bored me, people where I lived didn't excite me. Conversations about T.V. and what's being cooked for dinner didn't really float my boat. I found myself getting antsy with them, it wasn't their fault. It was me, things that excite and entice women my age like getting a new stair carpet, mowing a lawn, or watching mind numbing TV just didn't appeal to me. No one understood. I just couldn't describe it to anyone who understood.

People who really know me know I need something exciting. I felt I'd lost my purpose in life.

Life was pretty much defined by what new dress I'd got – and there were lots of them – or how clean my house was (not very). I was depressed – really depressed.

I had no one to talk to, the childhood me was bohemian and different and didn't care. The grown up me was boring and bored.

It was about this time I decided to try online dating again.

Chapter 16
Arriving in Nepal

I arrived in Kathmandu. The airport appeared to be kitted out like our local Thai restaurant with panelled wood walls and Buddha pictures everywhere. It was dark and dingy, like being in the 1960's without the miniskirts and cool music.

I didn't hold much hope for the Wi-Fi here. I turned my phone on to try and find some sort of instructions for my onward travel. Wi-Fi did exist and the icon was coming up, this prospect excited me more than a new land.

I tried and tried, and I couldn't access the Wi-Fi.

Oh no! What would I do for two weeks? I couldn't last 2 minutes without Wi-Fi.

Nervous anxiety and I were settling in nicely, I could feel my chest getting tight with panic. I wanted to WhatsApp everyone and tell them I'd arrived and that the flight hadn't killed me.

I told myself I'm a grownup woman and I've spent more than half my life without the internet, why couldn't I cope for a few weeks? Unfortunately, I am a twenty-first century woman. In some instances, like chatting up twenty or thirty something toy-boys and gallivanting halfway around the world solo, it worked for me. In others, like my addiction for immediacy and technology, it didn't.

I did have a female friend who was slightly younger and had never used the internet, she didn't have a social media account and didn't own a smartphone. I found it endearing if not a bit old fashioned and odd. My life pretty much revolved around the internet and social media.

I queued up to get my Nepali visa, which took an age to sort out. I went to grab some currency, but that took 30 minutes to sign multiple papers, and I had go a very long queue twice. Once to verify who I was and second to get the bloody money. The joys of going to a country with a closed currency.

I headed to get my backpack, that dreaded heavy monstrosity that I hadn't seen since Birmingham.

Then a panic pang hit me like a bolt of lightning.

'Where the heck was I going? Who was meeting me? What was the plan? Aren't there more volunteers?'
Everyone seemed to have a destination and pick point except me. Walking tours, hospital volunteers, and missionaries.
I have to admit, after four days of travelling to this place I had no clue about my final destination. I hadn't read any of the e-mails that the charity sent, and I couldn't get on Wi-Fi to check. I hadn't participated in any of the Facebook groups because it was meant to be an adventure.

'But what will I do if no one collects me? I was nearly four hours late; they might have been and gone, leaving me to fend for myself'. The negative thoughts ran around in my head, making me feel a bit sick.

'Come on Elise, Mrs Contingency Woman extraordinaire, what's your plan now, you idiot?' I said to myself.

There was no plan. I hadn't thought about it at all.

I wandered around the airport looking for people. My palms were sweaty, my body sluggish, I had blisters pulsating on my ankles from my walk around Delhi the day before.
I was so tired I forgot the name of the company I was working for. I couldn't access Facebook, even to try logging into the group. Anxiety built up inside me and overcame me causing my heart to race faster and faster.

Where were the English people? Everyone seemed foreign and the signs were like hieroglyphics, obviously they weren't, they were Nepali. Nepali? Hieroglyphics? All the same to me at this point.

I didn't want to speak, I just wanted to cry. *'Pull yourself together you stupid cow; you're an adult for goodness sake!'*, I told myself as I walked outside desperately looking around for someone to help me.
The dusky mid-day sun warmed my skin and all I could see was groups of faces, different types of faces. Faces holding up cards, faces smiling to meet their relatives and, like India, predominantly men.

I overheard a group of Italians – relief at last a European language. At least I could understand a bit of what was said.
"Scusi!" I yelped holding up my hand for attention, in desperation like a lost puppy wanting it's Mum.
One turned around as if they'd heard me, but then they disappeared. I got swept up in the hustle and bustle of crowds outside the airport and away they went by taxi. I was left listening to the prattling noise in an unfamiliar language.
All the time I was thinking once again, 'Contingency, contingency, what's the backup plan? What bloody backup plan? Come on Elise, there's got to be a plan B'.

'Where's the old Elise? The Elise who went off to Italy to work at twenty-one? She's in there somewhere. Elise the brave, Elise the explorer, come on and channel that Elise', I chanted to my subconscious mind, in hope of dragging the old me out.
The twenty-one-year-old Elise was wide-eyed and excited, she hadn't experienced disappointment. I needed her to rise her head and come out today.

I think I briefly read something about going to a hostel if no one turned up to collect you. A hostel! I've never stayed in a hostel in my life.

Aren't they full of druggies and prostitutes? Why didn't I read the stuff they sent? I would have had at least a name and a fighting chance of survival in this hell hole. I hated Nepal already. I was scared once again, well and truly out of my comfort zone. Nepal wasn't zen at all, it was like Delhi only without any English signs.

I thought, 'I'll get the next flight to Dubai. I've got friends in Dubai'.

I ran over to the desk,

"Excuse me, do you speak English?"

"*A little bit,*" said the woman behind the counter.

"What time is the next flight to Dubai?" I said, hopeful.

"*9 o'clock,*" said the woman.

"Fabulous that gives me 5 hours in the airport," I said looking at the time on my phone.

"9am tomorrow not 9pm today," she said shaking her head.

"Oh."

I dragged my luggage outside, looking sad and vulnerable in the hope someone would take pity on me. This tactic worked when I was touring around Italy. I once got a free taxi in Palermo all because the cute driver wanted a kiss on the cheek. I was happy to oblige if it saved me a few Lira.

Now, middle aged and not quite as cute, it didn't work at all. No one wanted to kiss me or offer me a free anything.

"Mrs Kaye!" I heard a voice shout, "I am Yubaraj from original volunteers."

A young and handsome man shouted at me from across the carpark. He looked friendly and cute, and I think I quite fancied him – maybe I was just happy to see a friendly face. I think I just fancied any man who showed me any sort of attention.

"I recognised you from your passport details," he continued.

Oh dear, I look like I've been dug up and stuffed on my passport and my hair is short, I muttered under my breath.

"Oh yes, of course, original volunteers, yes that's right," I said disorientated.

"Mrs Kaye, you follow me to the car," he said hurrying me into the taxi containing a very stern looking driver and a passenger I perceived to be his son.

Who knows, it was probably his mate who needed a lift to the shops on the route. I later found out that dropping and picking random people up was the norm over there. Turning a 30 minute journey into a 2 hour one.
Yubaraj was a chatterbox, he was full of facts telling me about this and that, he was attempting to engage with me.
I wasn't a chatterbox today, and I wasn't really listening, in fact, he was irritating me slightly. I was so tired and grumpy that I actually wanted to rip his chatty little head off.

I was miserable, tired, and bloated from flying. I'd never mastered the art of looking glamorous on a flight. Even when I flew business class in the old days, I'd get on the plane looking like a film star and leave the plane looking like I'd had a combination of a mid-air boxing match and a food fight. Black, mascara smudged eyes, lipstick halfway up my face, bloated face, swollen legs, and dry skin – not to mention food stuck in my hair. I'd always arrive at my destination looking like I needed a good bath and sleep.

Landing in Nepal, I was a bit hungry, and very much looking forward to sampling some Nepali food that I'd heard so much about from some of my friends.

After a chaotic trip across Kathmandu, Yubaraj announced I'd be staying the night in at some guy called Asim's house. I suppose if I'd read the blurb they'd sent me I would have known all about Asim and I wouldn't have felt hesitant about being there.

Asim and his family lived in 3 storey property on the west side of Kathmandu. The house was plush with beautiful rich textiles. Deep red and gold curtains, beautifully crafted rugs of similar colours with mahogany cabinets and sideboards. A statue of the Hindu god Shiva was situated on a plinth in the corner of the room. I hadn't realised Nepali people were Hindu and I'd assumed Asim was an Islamic name based on the very potted knowledge of Asian culture and religions I'd picked up from working in other countries.

Asim and his wife weren't there, and the house seemed to be run by 13 year old school girl called Nani. She made me dinner, and I had my first taste of Nepali food – real Nepali food, not the stuff served in UK restaurants. It was at this meal I was first acquainted with Daal Baat. A lentil and rice concoction favoured by Nepali people and the staple diet in Nepal. It was nice, but I wasn't sure I'd rush out to a restaurant to order it though.

The tiled floors were gleamingly polished, probably by Nani. This house was beautiful and not at all a reflection of the Nepali society I'd seen on my hour-long journey across the city from the airport. Yubaraj assured me I would be going to the Orphanage tomorrow and I could start work. But before I did, there was a cultural induction to go through. I was eager to get stuck in and meet the Orphans.

Chapter 17
Meeting Liam

After the disaster of paying for online dating, I decided to give Tinder another shot, at least they weren't gargoyles. Knob head and idiots yes, but not ugly. Tinder was a player's playground, and I needed some fun in my miserable life.

I uploaded some new pictures – slightly slimmer, prettier ones. I wasn't smiling on any of them. I hadn't smiled for a while.

I'd connected with a guy online who looked quite cute, not out of my league gorgeous like the model, but cute and enough to keep my interest. He was a junior doctor, 10 years younger than me, or so it said on Tinder.

I have to be honest, the thought of someone in the caring professional excited me, the thought of him being 10 years younger excited me even more.

I'm not sure why it excited me as I imagined most of the day, he was either sitting in or dealing with bodily fluids. I thought as he must see some disgusting sights so my body wouldn't put him off.

I showed my mates his picture and they agreed he was gorgeous, but they also cautioned me not to get too attached, as he looked like a cheeky player.

"Keep away from him Elise, why do you always go for looks?" one friend said.

"He looks naughty, he'll break your heart and there's not much left it as it is," said another.

"I can't go out with an ugly guy, I'm sorry, I'd rather stay single," I said in a huff.

"Elise, if we all fancy him, so will half of Birmingham. He'll love himself far more than he'll ever love you, this will end in tears, stay clear of him," another friend said.

"I've been out with better looking guys," I said on the defence.
 Yeah, look how those relationships ended. Plus, you're getting on a bit now, you need to lower your standards in the looks department," another friend chipped in.

Disgusted with the lack of support from my friends and half wanting to prove to them I was still gorgeous and fanciable, I started to text him.

I sent my first text and waited in anticipation. Within minutes, he sent me a text me back. We continued to text for days, long lengthy texts, and he seemed to respond to my wit and was equally witty.
He was bouncy and fun on his messages. He had an energy I can't even begin to describe. I was excited by his messages and for the first time in ages I had a smile on my face. For the first time since online dating I wasn't asked for pictures of my boobs or he didn't send me any of his genitalia. Quite refreshing really. He was down to earth but classy not coarse as others had been.

I used all my best jokes and found myself being bloody hilarious. I used innuendos that he just 'got'. If I had a £1 for every time I mentioned him giving me a check-up and thermometers, I'd be very rich. I was so hilarious, and I felt like the most exciting person on earth, not the washed-up old girl I'd felt since Steve had gone.

He was cheeky and just got me (something which most men didn't). At first, I thought he was trying too hard, as he seemed to like everything I did. But I felt at ease with him and didn't need to pretend to be anything. We shared a love of travel and our texts went on for ages as we flipped between multiple subjects and photographs from our holidays. He was wild and sweet and exciting. He made me feel young again.

He made me feel alive and sexy. So, I took the plunge and booked a hotel room in town. This could have gone disastrously wrong, but I used my intuition that it was safe. I also stalked the shit out of him on social media prior to meeting, just to ensure he was genuine.

We agreed to meet in the hotel bar. I was so scared he wouldn't turn up or that I wouldn't connect with him as we had done on text, After all, the last twelve months had been one disappointment after another. But I was really looking forward to meeting him and having some fun.

Something came over me and I had some compelling reason to be alluring. The guy had brought out the inner vamp in me. I hadn't felt like this for such a long time and whatever happened after this date I'd be eternally grateful for him unleashing my latent almost dead sex appeal.

I didn't know whether it was because of him, but I felt compelled to buy a pair of Louboutin shoes. I'd always wanted a pair of the red soled beauties adorning my feet but didn't know where I'd wear them. As I entered the shoe department in Harvey Nicols, my heart was pumping in anticipation. I spotted what I wanted, a pair of emerald green heels with mini gold spikes on them, very dominatrix. I looked at the price tag - £600!

£600 for a pair of shoes, but if they made me feel sexy again, they were worth every penny.

I lifted them up and I could smell the leather, the newness of those beautifully crafted green swede heels.

I placed them on my feet and walked around the store. They made my calf look slim, my bum look pert, and gave me height. I was hot in these heels!

Imagine the heels and my red underwear- Wow!

I checked into my room and I carefully unwrapped my new shoes, I was going to have one hell of a night in these I told myself.

'*Ping!*' I received a text from him saying he was running late and he couldn't get parked. It was a dark, quiet Sunday night in February and I'm sure he was lying to me. Half expecting him to stand me up and half expecting him to disappoint.

Just as I was getting caught up in my negativity from the past year, a text pops up and it was him.

'Hi, it's me! I'm in the bar downstairs.'

I walked into the dimly lit hotel bar in my gorgeous new shoes, my black mac, and red underwear underneath. *'Oh my god! What if I don't fancy him? What if he's a wanker? What if someone else wrote those messages?'* I mulled over in my head.

I walked through the corridor towards the bar and there he stood in front of me in his black coat and jeans. He wasn't quite as tall as I anticipated, but he wasn't short either – I was 4 inches taller than normal as I was wearing my Louboutin's. I looked him in the eye and my heart did a somersault. I felt it flutter before he even said a word. I walked over to him and looked him in the eyes again and was awestruck. No one had ever had that effect on me in my entire life, not even my husband. It was like I was face to face with my hero, a weird sensation filled my body. I looked at him ready to be my usual jovial self but couldn't speak. I opened my mouth to talk but nothing came out, just silent gaping.

He was the cutest thing I'd ever seen, and as soon as I laid my eyes on him it was like I'd seen those glistening eyes a million times before. His eyes looked blue in the dark of the hotel bar and they felt familiar, so weirdly familiar that looking him directly was uncomfortable.

His eyes made me want to cry in a massive emotional outburst. His smile was comforting and like one I'd known all my life. He made me feel like I was home where I belonged, my heart break melted, I knew he wasn't going to hurt me, not intentionally anyway. For the first time in a long time I felt at ease and my heart swelled. He gave me the same feeling I had for my daughter, an unconditional love. All this happened in a nano second and felt as if I was levitating, my soul was rising out of my body.

"Well, you take a shit photo," I said emphasising the *you*, meaning he was better looking in real life.

"Very charming, well thank you, too!" he said.

"I...I mean you're gorgeous," I stuttered, hoping my upfront no nonsense Yorkshire-ness hadn't offended.

He knew exactly what I meant and looked at me slowly, examining me.
I dived in and kissed him passionately on the lips and hugged him so tightly I thought he would burst, he was taken aback by my sexual advances.

"Well at least let me take my coat off before you rape me, you div," he said in his light Brummie accent.

"Oops sorry, it's been a while," I awkwardly apologised. But there was nothing awkward about this connection, it was natural, and my kiss felt like I was greeting an old lover.

I lead him to the hotel lift and continued to kiss him passionately.

"Aren't we going for a drink?" he said nervously.

"What do you want to do?" I replied, almost dragging him in the room.

We kissed and kissed and kissed, he was such a passionate kisser, almost Latin in his approach. I had kissed a few Latin boys in my pre-marriage times.

In my dimly lit, dark wooden room, we came up for air and had a good chat about travel, family, and anything. I didn't need to put on an act. I sat on his lap in a very skimpy dress revealing my red underwear like I'd done a million times before. I chatted to him like he knew my family and I his, like old mates catching up after years apart.

"Do you like my shoes? They're Louboutin's!" I said showing off. "They were £600!" I boasted.

"I don't even know what they are, but that seems a lot of money for a pair of shoes, and more than a week's wages for most people," he answered back not particularly impressed by my overpriced purchase.

"Do you like them?" I asked like a school girl waiting to hear she'd passed an exam.

"Yeah, nice," he replied in a nonchalant way, disinterested in such excess, as he leaned in to kiss me.

I continued to let him kiss me. At first, he seemed embarrassed, but then he let loose and became more and more passionate, touching me gently and lightly on my thighs.
I'm an imposing character when aroused, some may say overbearing, so I wasn't surprised at his semi-fear, semi-intrigued contorted face. He stared at me like he was obsessed. I moved over to the table to pour a drink of prosecco, I could feel his eyes following me, following my every move and his mouth gaping open like an awestruck teenager.

I gulped my drink and he moved forward gently kissing my neck.

I stood static, while he slowly moved his lips down my body, and I tingled all over.

116

He unclasped my bra and placed me on the bed still kissing me. He lightly touched my ankles, then my legs covering me with small kisses. Moving slowly up my body, kissing my calf, my thigh, my bum, and biting my bum gently until he reached my inner thigh. He kissed my inner thigh and I re-coiled with pleasure.

Then he carefully pulled down my red lace pants and opened my legs, he moved his kisses along towards my pussy, putting his tongue inside me, back and forth and making me spasm and groan with every move. He moved his tongue back and forth along my clit and slowly inserted his fingers inside me while continuing to flick my clit with his tongue. All the time I kept my green spiked Louboutin shoes on. This was ecstasy like I'd never known. This boy was good, he was attentive and was determined for me to have a good time.

He continued to pleasure me with his tongue until I climaxed and lay back with my legs open, satisfied. The shoes might have been £600 but they gave me sex appeal and I'd wear them all over again.

I returned the favour and gave him one of my epic blow jobs. He didn't complain, and I know he enjoyed it as within minutes with were making love.

I wouldn't normally use the term 'making love' but in this instance that's what it felt like.

I'd had lots of sex before, but nothing had prepared me for this out of body experience.

We talked and joked some more, ignoring what had just happened. I was in heaven and wanted it to happen all over again, this was the best night I could remember in my sexual maturity years.

"Well as you know my Dad's had a terrible time lately," I said, like he and my dad were acquainted.

He never corrected me, he continued engaging in conversation with familiarity.

It was an odd experience and one I'll never tire of re-living. I babbled away without a pause and then when it was his turn to speak, I hung on his every word like fascinated teenager. We bounced off each other and finished each other's sentences.

The adoration I felt in my heart was unbelievable, like it had opened up and I was floating on a cloud, particularly as he hadn't said anything particularly remarkable.

Why was I drawn to this guy? Did he just have good pheromones as one friend would describe it. This guy didn't just have good pheromones, he had amazing pheromones – drug addict style pheromones.

I was a bit drunk the first time we met; I needed the courage in case it all went wrong as so many dates before it had. I didn't forget a word he said.

A good test of my interest in someone is if I remember every word they say.

He was a fair bit younger than me, ex-army, had served in Afghanistan, and now a junior doctor. He excited me and I liked talking to him like as a friend – helped by the fact he was beautiful. I was in love with him, head over heels in love with him. I told myself this was ridiculous I'd known the guy minutes, but I was in love.

We chatted and kissed, we touched each other lightly then hurriedly as we became more passionate. He kissed me all over my body and stroked me lightly. Sex with Liam was like a scene from a film, the type of sex I craved. He didn't speak much he just knew how and where to touch me. This on on/off passion lasted for hours and I didn't want it to stop.

There was one problem; Liam was a player, I didn't know for certain, but I could just tell.

He was very experienced with women, too good in bed not to be.

He worked with the public so there was a lot of opportunity to meet women. Not that I'm suggesting he'd shag his patients, particularly working in A&E, that would be wrong, but the guy knew exactly what he was doing.

He knew how to charm women and was bloody good at it. It worked on me and bearing in mind I was the Ice Queen with men at this point, he melted my hard heart and made me feel special.

I made a comment about my stomach – something I'd hated since having Sophia. He said,

"You've earned that, and you've got something lovely as a result!"

My heart lifted what a lovely reaction.

I was still suspicious as usual, but that comment was sweet, and he was right. I might have had a bit of a tummy, but I had earned it. This is something I still think about as I have pangs of self-doubt. He'll never know the effect that wonderful comment had on me. I'd thought about it as several months before Steve had convinced me to go for a tummy tuck. I'd had numerous consultations and was ready to go and have the operation when I bottled it and decided to try and exercise instead.

The night was wonderful, and we agreed to meet again, although I wasn't sure if he was really that bothered. We messaged for a while afterwards, but I wasn't ready to get my heart broken again and he would almost certainly do that.

I stopped messaging back and started to ignore him, little did I know that this was a pattern I became all too familiar with in my relationships.

119

Chapter 18
Leaving Kathmandon't

Then next day, I woke up to a slightly smoggy view of the low lying Himalayas. Yubaraj had suggested I go up to the roof terrace of Asim's house and take a look at the sights from a higher level.
I still couldn't believe I was there in Everest country; I had to pinch myself. It wasn't my usual Christmas view. It usually rained at Christmas in Staffordshire, home was definitely less populated and quieter, bordering on boring.
The view was one of two halves; I could see a buzzing metropolis of high-rise buildings and busy streets strewn with people right under my nose. When I looked out, there were a stunning range of snow topped mountains over the horizon.

My first lesson for the day; apparently a mountain is only mountain if it has snow otherwise it's just a hill. There were a lot of mountains from what I could make out under the hazy grey of pollution that blanketed Kathmandu that morning. I could see Everest in the distance – I convincingly told myself, although I'm not sure I could from this part of Kathmandu. I'll embellish that bit, no one will know unless reading this you happen to be a mountain expert.
The Nepali people I'd met so far were warm, friendly, and very hospitable. Although Yubaraj, Nani, and my driver were hardly a good sample size of the entire population of a country, I had a good vibe and I was all about going with the positive vibes nowadays.
Nani taught me to make Nepalese tea using black salt and tea leaves. It was a beautiful earl grey tasting tea made from Nepali tea leaves, black Himalayan salt (not the pink stuff you get in Waitrose), pepper, a sugar cube and water. The black pepper and salt gave it a spicy but saline taste and one I won't forget. I loved it and tried to make it on my own when I came back home, but to no avail.
She made me an omelette because she thought I'd prefer an English breakfast rather than Daal again, I was about to find out that Daal Baat is every meal. I savoured that omelette and she used the same

Himalayan black salt she's used in the tea, giving it a spicy almost peppery and salty kick.

I had a chat with her, and she had been an orphan at the girl's orphanage in Chitwan. I explained that I was going to go there. She said I'd love it and the national park nearby was stunning.

The truth was, I didn't know where I was going as Asim had loads of projects he supported. I'd seen promotional material about Chitwan and assumed that's where I'd be going.

Asim and his family liked Nani's attitude and hard work, so she lived with the family as a housekeeper. She was very mature for a 13yr old girl.

Her English was good, and she was well educated and had excellent manners. With improved status and education, she hoped to meet a better class of husband and have a family in a few years time. The sarcastic bitch in my head was saying *'I'd had a decent education and my manners were good apart from the occasional swear word, but it didn't get me a decent husband'*. In fact, my education and social awareness just made me a magnet for arseholes and love repressed manipulative dickheads. I hope Nani had more luck than I did in finding love.

"That's so lovely," I said, "and make sure he provides for you and your children," I said to her in a motherly voice.

I had a 17-year-old niece who I loved to bits. She was more bothered about which top to buy from New Look or whether her Mum would get her some new straighteners for Christmas. Here in the middle of Kathmandu was 13-year-old Nani considering marriage and children. Marriage in Nepal was about security and future proofing; it was fundamentally survival, everything seemed to be about survival. My situation seemed pathetic and temporary in comparison. My depression seemed so insignificant and my suicide contemplation was just self-absorbed attention seeking. It seemed real at the time but in Nepal where life was precious and amenities were scarce, I felt a fool for even considering it.

121

I fully understand people who slide into a deep depression and want to take their lives, but I urge them to try something different, drag out the last scrap of energy and try making it work, try something different. Life is never that bad in the long term.

After breakfast, I explored Kathmandu then visited some Buddhist temples all under the expert guidance of the very lovely Yubaraj. I liked Yubaraj, he was about 5ft 7, dark skin, and almost certainly of Indian heritage, with a nice open smiley face. He had a very western attitude and excellent colloquial English although he had never been to the UK. He asked about my husband and didn't bat an eyelid when I told him I was getting divorced - something he'd done and had remarried a few years ago. This was an absolute rarity in Nepali culture, he seemed a bit ashamed he was divorced from his first wife, she had mental health issues and wasn't able to commit to their marriage.

He was empathetic to my situation and didn't make me feel like an outcast at least. I knew as I ventured more towards the countryside to work, people would not share the same sentiment as him. For a second, we had something in common. I'd warmed to him. I didn't feel alien or humiliated by being a virtually divorced woman travelling Asia, and I wouldn't be the first and certainly not the last.

We visited Boudhanath, a beautiful white Stupa. A Stupa is a hemispherical structure containing remains of Buddhist monks and nuns. Like a gigantic mausoleum only less macabre and more peaceful. These are used as a place of meditation for those practising the Buddhist faith. Little eyes and a nose painted on the tower on top of dome seemed to smile at me wishing me a good day; I was having a fabulous day thank you Mr Winking Stupa, my day was just fabulous.

Next on the city tour was Pashupatinath temple in the centre of the city, and I learned about how Hinduism and Buddhism are combined in Nepal.

I lit a incense stick and said a little prayer;

'Please God, if there is one, please make the bullshit end when I return to the UK'.

I'm not sure that was the right language to use in front of Buddha. They'd been a lot going on, so I'm sure he would understand.

Don't let the guidebook fool you, it wasn't a gratifying experience, not when there were wild monkeys everywhere jumping out at me in an attempt to scratch and attack.
I like chimps, but those wiry little monkeys scare me, multiples of any animals scare me. Like a scene from Alfred Hitchcock's, 'The Birds' or worst still the film 'Outbreak' with Dustin Hoffman. Those scratchy, potentially diseased evil monkeys frightened me more than the Kathmandu traffic, and that was horrific.
I then went to the volunteer office. It wasn't an office, more of a scene from a Russian war film. All grey with concrete walls, a thread bear rug on the cold hard floor and just for decoration, a map of the world on the wall behind a battered old wooden desk.
I was half expecting a Bond Villain to twizzle a chair around from behind the desk and say *I've been expecting you Mrs Kaye* in a sinister voice while holding on to a goat. It wouldn't be a cat; a goat was more Nepali. The Nepali people couldn't be sinister if they tried and the goat image made everything seem more jovial.

We'd been in town a long time and I was dying for a wee. I made the mistake of asking for the toilet. A dirty porcelain hole which smelled like the gents in a nightclub at 4am on a Sunday morning. The stinky stench was hitting the back of my throat and stinging as I gulped it down and crouched over it, trying not to pee on my leg and down my leggings. Leggings I was about to be wearing for another few days.
I had my culture training in a room next to the office and learnt some of Nepali language with Yubaraj. I was so tired, I couldn't remember anything other than Namaste, and I learnt that word before I came from my meditation app.

We shared photos of our daughters. He showed me a picture of his new wife and we talked a lot about Nepali culture and customs. I was never going to remember any of them but was told it was important as I would be judged on my ability to install these in the orphans. That afternoon I did the school run for Asim's sons. A one-hour trip across the city and a half an hour wait at the police school, which I later found out the boys weren't fans of. I'll never moan again about our school run. It was hell, dodging cars, cramped up in a red-hot jeep, surrounded by cases and shopping bags.

We stopped several times to pick up and drop off various members of the driver's family on the way to the shops. None of them speaking to me, just in Nepali.

The boys made the driver stop on the way home to get samosas because the oldest one was starving. They gave me a samosa, which was a lucky escape from Daal Baat. I savoured the samosa not knowing when I'd get another Daal Baat break.

The next day I was to be up at 5am to get the seven - potentially ten - hour depending on the roads) bus ride to Pokhara to the orphanage. I wasn't going to the Chitwan one as I'd anticipated. I'd say bye to Yubaraj and Hello Tikka who was going to be my guide. I hoped Tikka would have the same sense of humour. Yubaraj had been funny and sarcastic.

'Jiskeko' was the word of the day in Kathmandu ' *—just kidding'*. One more word retained in my Nepali vocabulary.

As we left the busy run-down streets of Kathmandon't, my new name for Kathmandu, I felt relief and a sense of spring. Kathmandu hadn't grabbed me like I thought it would.

Too cold, too dank, too dirty, and far too busy.

I had a sensation of spring after a harsh, cold winter. Relief after an arduous journey. Like some Lara Croft tomb raider character, I'd battled grime, traffic, fire, sexual advances, and worst of all a marriage break up. But finally, I was almost there, on the edge of a peaceful land. Peace was what I came for, and peace was what I was going bloody well have. I knew my experience at the orphanage was going to be a special one, I had positive vibes.

I was keen to get started because Yubaraj had informed me my placement was in a beautiful location by a lake and near the mountains.

The journey was long and boring but also stunningly beautiful and I felt myself lucky to be there. I could quite easily spend the holiday by the pool in an all-inclusive resort in Tenerife.

Chapter 19
Liam Returns

For six months I didn't contact Liam, I had more disastrous dates. I got pissed and cried on many outings with men, was walked out on by a football coach, called weird - there were late night calls and tearsm and I just got bored with dates. There were suggestive texts and more ab and genital pictures. I kept thinking, if this is dating, I'll stay single. Liam had been the only one I got on with and although we had minimal contact, I really liked him. He was my favourite out of all the idiots I'd dated, and he was sweet and funny too. I knew at the very least we got on as friends.

Prompted by my friend Sarah, I contacted him again and of course he was his usual bubbly self. Like a bouncy little Peter Pan who never seemed phased by anything. We decided to meet for lunch (originally dinner but true to form, he cancelled that). He always let me down but for some strange reason I knew it wasn't deliberate. He had stuff to deal with, stuff he never told. He didn't need to tell me, I just knew. I can be a head strong independent person who doesn't give second chances; but when I'm hooked, I'm hooked. For some compelling reason I always forgave Liam. I forgave him for cancelling on me and for not returning my messages. Why? because I think he's like me, he's a deep soul, and like me he's a disorganised dope and he forgets, he always forgets. Not because he's rude, because life just gets in the way. He juggles too many things and can't prioritise. He's immature and non-committal and any form of organisation sends him running. I always say it's like looking in a mirror, although I'm sexier with bigger boobs.

We met and, as usual, had a laugh. I'd feigned some excuse about wanting to develop an app, which at the time was partially true. He sat and let me pitch ideas to him like a poor man's Dragons Den, only this was in Nando's with a coke and a chicken pitta. I didn't drink with Liam; he didn't like me drinking.

126

I really wanted to check out if he was as creative as I thought he was and see if we were on the same wavelength. The truth was I just wanted to see him, to touch him, to let him hug me. I was lonely and I wanted him to cure my loneliness.

He also had ideas too and the pair of us talked and talked about how they'd work. Which ideas neither of us liked. The flow of conversation was easy like we'd always known each other. Like we were old mates picking up where we'd left off. We were always like this, old mates picking up where we left off.

At times he looked distracted but not by our surroundings, by me. He looked at me like I was an angel, all wide eyed and awesome, he looked mesmerised. He never took his eyes off mine. I may have been wrong, but I think he did like me, I was sure he admired me.

It was quite arousing. He joked that I needed a nice junior doctor in my life. I told him I needed to stop dating young boys. He said,

"I'm not a boy, I'm a man!"

I smiled and agreed, he was now he was over 30. We laughed together catching each other's eyes, my heart leapt. He sighed, a long drawn out sigh, like a child who was told they couldn't have the sweets they were lusting over.

But he could have me, I just was too scared to tell him.

The moment broke and we snapped into reality, announcing he had to go and meet his new girlfriend.

"She's a nice girl you know Els, very pretty," he said.

"And why wouldn't she be? You're an attractive nice guy, I'm happy for you," I said holding back the tears.

He gave me an awkward hug and left.

Crestfallen I let out a tear. It's difficult to explain such a massive emotional surge having only met the guy twice. But his presence hit every cell in my body and could bring out spontaneous emotions in me.

I sat there nursing my coffee for another 30mins thinking;

Why did he agree to meet if he didn't care?

Why did he agree to meet knowing he had a girlfriend now?

Was he hedging his bets, and playing me? I didn't want to be played anymore; I was sick of being played.

I walked back to the car park with a mix of emotions. Happy, frustrated, and sad. Surprisingly not jealous of his girlfriend. Something told me that we had a special relationship that no girlfriend would have with him.
He left it three months (his usual style) then I got a message asking if he could come to my new house. It actually said,

"I better come round and see this nice new house of yours, hadn't I Bab?"

Like he should come because he was an old mate who wanted to see me doing well. But he wasn't, he was a guy I'd met online twice.
We agreed a day and I waited but as usual he let me down. He was in the area, but he had things to deal with at home. The next time I saw him was a week after he'd let me down. He was supposed to come around and he didn't due to some drama with his house mates, which I did help him sort out.
I was in my forties, a woman with my own home and a child, and he had housemates. What part of this deal did I think was going to work? If he did want a relationship would he be able to commit? I was over thinking the situation far too much. I wasn't overthinking my feelings though; they were very real.

He decided he was going to come and see my new house. He announced he was coming over on a Monday afternoon. True to form he was late and a got a panicky text saying the traffic was bad. I called him a disorganised div. Smiling to myself I could see so many of my characteristics in him, I found it endearing. Even his annoying habits made me smile. He didn't mean to be like this, it was just the way he was.

He turned up letting himself in, bold as brass like he'd been there before. Even my friends knock the door. He had a northern way about him. His cockiness and confident attitude, down to earth personality, familiar with everyone. I could relate, but underneath there was a sensitive soul.

I saw his big smiley face and gorgeous green eyes, which made me beam too. His cheeky smile lit up any bad day.

I joked with him that his smile should be prescribed on the NHS, and I suppose in a way it was.

We chatted with ease as usual and he helped me cook lunch.

I gave him a facial treatment with my new ultrasound facial machine. He had a pimple on his chin so asked me to look at it. There was an intense moment where I was touching him, it felt so natural like we always do this stuff and I could feel my spine tingling, it was very sensual. Every nerve in my body tingled and I could tell he felt it too. It was a feeling of ecstasy. He didn't need to touch me, as just thinking about him would trigger the same response.

He broke the moment, pulled away and said awkwardly;

*"I can do it myself now, thank **you**,"* with a strong emphasis on 'you'.

We ate lunch and he was telling me about his trip to Thailand. I talked about my ex and cried as I always did.

"Don't bloody cry Els, I can't cope with you crying," he said.

I joked that he must be crap at work then as people must cry all the time.

129

'Shall I just give you a blood transfusion Mrs Evans, you might die, but for God's sake don't bloody cry, I can't cope with crying," I joked as I took the piss out of him with his patients.

He laughed and called me a Dingbat, a phrase I hadn't heard since I was twelve. I liked it, it made me feel like a child again.

He talked about his girlfriend and I could feel myself welling up again, so I distracted the situation by making a coffee and faffing about moving things around the kitchen – my trade mark deflection tactic. He said she was a nice girl very beautiful and he was hoping that he wouldn't mess this relationship up. Again I did the honourable thing and said;

"Of course she's a nice girl Liam, she's with you. And no, don't mess it up. At least try and make a go of this one."

I secretly wanted him to mess it up, but I also wanted him to be happy, and if she made him happy then that was ok. I think very grown up of me too, considering how immature I'd been about Steve's affair. I was being the bigger person once again, but the bigger person was throwing my mental health into disarray.

Lusting over Liam was consuming me.

There was a moment while he sat in my office listening to music and I sat on the floor. A song came on and he closed his eyes. I stayed quiet but could feel his heart vibrating. Up until this point we had been noisily joking and chatting away.

It was an intimate moment but without either of us touching. I felt loved for the first time in ages, my heart flipped and it felt like it was opening. It takes a lot for my heart to flip, but he does it. Putting things into perspective at this point I'd been out on over 30 dates and not one of them made me feel like he made me feel.

The song finished and we carried on as usual talking about our travels and joking about.

After 4 hours of chatting, spot squeezing, and quiet lustful looks – maybe I imagined that – he left. Never once did he try to touch me or kiss me. I wanted him to, but he didn't.

He had before, we'd been intimate on one occasion, before the girlfriend came along and before I decided to ignore him.

I really wanted him to look into my eyes, hold my face in his hands and slowly kiss me.

I wanted passion and intrigue and to feel loved.

As he left, he hugged me. The hug this time wasn't awkward, it was like a caress that lingered a while. He didn't do anything to step over the mark or betray his girlfriend, but I knew that hug was more than just mates. This guy was in love with me, I was convinced. My intuition was in overdrive and knew he was the one.

He disappeared and said he'd see me in January some three months later. I didn't understand him, he gave me a hug like that and then said he'd see me in three months! These weren't the actions of a player but scared young man who was confused. Like he wasn't quite ready to play with the grown-ups but desperately wanting to. Just teetering on the edge. Ours was a spiritual connection, I knew because I had never experienced anything like it before. I'd been married for years and I was no stranger to dating and never had I felt like this.

I was convinced he was in my life for a specific purpose and didn't know what that purpose was. All I recalled was a dream I'd had in 2003 about a Doctor and an army man, I kidded myself thinking he was the man from my distant dream.

I was so frustrated and fed up with this cat and mouse game that I decided to put an end to it. I'd know the guy a year and it seemed to be going nowhere. He was too busy distracting himself with work and his beautiful girlfriend.

So, what I did next was absolutely ridiculous, but I don't regret a thing.

Convinced he really liked me – possibly even loved me – I wrote to him a long lengthy old school style letter:

"To Mr Almost Amazing,

Here's your face iron to make you look pretty on the TV.

Have an amazing time in Thailand and please keep safe.

I'm gonna say this now or I'm not being honest with you – I bloody love you!

Whatever happens from now on and however you react please know I really do love you.

If you feel the same let's go for it when you get back from Thailand.

Or alternatively I'll see you in 2037 when this has sunk in and I'm with someone else - you frustrating, amazing div!"

What possessed me? Midlife crisis? It was a bad move – or was it?

A couple of days later he sent a very lovely message saying thank you for the message and that I was going to hate him as he didn't have those feelings for me. He said I was an amazing person and my life was moving forwards while his was going backwards. He also said he wanted to make 'a go of it' with his girlfriend.
What does 'make a go of it' even mean? Steve had said it about the cleaner he'd gone off and had a baby with.
Was it a term used to hedge their bets or just to soften the blow, but neither of them wanted me?

Any other woman in my position would have died from shame knowing they had got it so wrong. I didn't feel embarrassment by this rejection, but I knew many of my friends would have been mortified.

"I'm sorry," I wrote. "I never want to see you again, please don't attempt to contact me I won't answer, and I don't hate you."

He texts back.
"Well I'll contact you. I don't want you out of my life, you're the only one who understands me, can we be friend

Chapter 20
The Long Road to Pokhara

I stepped onto the rickety looking bus and two things crossed my mind:

1) Was this death trap seriously going to make the seven – potentially nine – hour journey to Pokhara?

2) Where the hell were the toilets on this thing?

Both worried me, and the second thing worried me surprisingly more than the first. Besides; if I died on the way to Pokhara, I really wouldn't need to worry about needing a pee.

There were no toilets, and the more I thought about it, the more I needed to go. Any thought of anything liquid made my bladder swell, even looking at the bottle of water I'd stored in the footwell was starting to set me off.

Getting out of Kathmandu took about three hours and it was a hair-raising trip. The roads were churned up following the earthquake a few years before. Call me intuitive, but something told me that pre-disaster the roads weren't much better.

Nepali road infrastructure made Indian roads look Romanesque. Roads in Kathmandu were a series of concrete blocks with cracks in them and the rickety old bus tilted at a 90-degree angle as it navigated its way out of the city.

I felt like I was on the runaway train in a theme park, and I hate theme parks.

I sat next to a French girl who was working on behalf of the U.N. alongside her Dutch and Belgian colleagues. She was in her early twenties and seemed very much at home in Nepal. She explained that this was a tourist bus so slightly more palatial than your average Nepali bus. I looked around wondering what the normal Nepali buses were like for this to be deemed luxurious.

This bus was filthy with ripped seats and dirty windows, how bad could they get? I must have been spoilt back at Asim's house.
The French U.N girl also assured me there were toilet stops and lunch on route. Definitely worth the few extra rupees, I thought.

"Why are you in Nepal?" she asked me, I assumed she was waiting for an intelligent answer but not sure I had the resources to answer.
I thought for a second and replied,

"I honestly don't know."

"This place is like that, people come without knowing how or why they've come," said very sweetly replied. "They all want to help and be charitable, but it frustrates them because there's too much to do." She had a point, was travel the antidote of any washed-up person going through a midlife crisis? Crisis? Mine was more of an illness, an illness that had overwhelmed me and made me sad about a manipulative ex and fall in love with the wrong guy, the first guy who made me feel good - but he was still another wrong guy.
My reasons were different, my reasons were to help but also to help me. Medication hadn't worked, it just numbed my personality. Counselling was not helping, and if I'd stayed in Staffordshire I feared I would become an alcoholic or worst still, dead.
Dramatic I know, but I think I suffered a breakdown as I never felt the same again. It wasn't a psychologically diagnosed breakdown but being on the receiving end of emotional abuse and then falling for someone who was emotionally unavailable was bound to take its toll on anyone's mental health. I was an empathetic person, someone who absorbed energy like a sponge, whether it be good or bad.

We stopped in the middle of a mountain range both for toilets and to let people off. My French U.N. friend and her colleagues departed, and we wished each other well on our travels.
I went to the toilet. It's moments like these I longed for a 'she-wee' or face mask. The toilets were damp and dark, they smelled worse than

135

the office ones in Kathmandu and I could feel my mouth watering in a pre-vomit state. The smell was so bad, it made my nasal hairs sting. I pulled my hoody over my mouth as it spasmed ready to hurl. I held my breath as I crouched over the white ceramic shit stained hole in the ground avoiding skidding on urine and excrement, I inspected it too closely and could see some of the shit was so ingrained to the porcelain it looked like it had been lingering a while.

Once I got outside the toilet block, I let out the air I'd been holding in for 30 seconds. Relieved to have been to the toilet and more relieved to be out in the fresh air. I stepped back onto the bus and sank in my seat and fell asleep.

I dreamed a lot on the road to Pokhara: I thought about my trip so far and how it seemed a long time since I left my home. It had only been 5 days, but already sleepy Staffordshire seemed a long way away and it felt like I'd been gone forever.

Had I achieved what I wanted to yet?

Well, India had scared and inspired me. First tick in the box.

One of the things I wanted to do was to make people proud of me, and I wasn't sure I'd done that yet. Although some of my more stomach sensitive friends would've been proud at braving the shit stained toilets.

It was a lot about making people proud back home. I always seemed to be seeking approval from someone. I'd achieved and done a lot in life, mostly due to my determination and tenacity, but somehow, I still felt like a failure.

I felt like a failure because I'd surrounded myself with people who perpetuated that in me. Negativity always seemed to spur me on, and I wasn't happy unless I was competing with someone or responding to a call of 'I bet you can't do that'. My life up to now had been a series of events, competitions, and hobbies taken up to prove to others that I could do things, that I could succeed.

136

If I was a success, they would love me.

It was like climbing to the edge of the rainbow, I always got there only to find out the rainbow was made of flimsy shit and I'd spent the experience on my phone taking selfies, wanting approval and when I eventually did arrive, there was no pot of gold so the success was short lived. So, I carried on chasing rainbows. Rainbows that lead to constant disappointment.

I woke myself up dribbling and snoring. When I woke, we were in the middle of nowhere surrounded by snow-capped mountains. They didn't look real. I could almost touch them out of the window of the bus. The ride to Pokhara was a scary one. Hair-pin bends and no safety rails knowing that one wrong turn from the bus driver and we'd descend the ravine and into the valley below. It was a dramatic but perfectly reasonable fear.

In contrast to this terrifying concept the scenery was stunning, picture post card stunning. The jagged peaks, the alpine glaciers, the vastness of the range. I was in awe; I'd never seen such a beautiful wintery landscape. The sun shone against the glaciers and you could see fresh ice water trickling down the hillside and into the rivers below.

I drifted in and out of sleep state and at times didn't know if I was awake or dreaming. I'd travelled the world, but nothing prepared me for the awesomeness of the Himalayas.

Chapter 21
Revelations

I was dealing with the new normal. The new normal was a boring version of myself. Having no one to compete with was odd, but it was better than being controlled. It was refreshing not to give Steve a second thought and I could come and go as I pleased on the days that I didn't have Sophia.

Steve however, had other ideas. He would make attempts to control me by planting information on Sophia. I was paranoid about everything, I trusted no one because Steve always seemed to know where I was, who I was with, and what I was doing.

On the surface I was free but in reality, I was under the watchful eye of Steve and his spies.

It was like he was one step ahead. When a hole appeared in my skirting board and a set of keys went missing from the kitchen drawer, I'd convinced myself he'd planted a camera and was watching me. I was driving myself crazy with paranoia and didn't trust anyone, including Sophia.

I was running a little business selling cosmetic teeth whitening and facial treatments and kept it quite low key, although even Steve seemed to know about that too. He used it as ammunition against me in the divorce settlement, as if whitening a few people's teeth was going to turn me into a billionaire.

Out of the blue, Jason, a friend of Steve's, messaged me asking if he could have his teeth done for his up and coming wedding.

Jason was an old friend of Steve's and they'd spent many a Friday night out on the town together. They'd been very good mates a few years ago but then they stopped going out. Their friendship had ground to a halt and Steve had no one to go out with.

I wondered why their friendship had ended, and I never questioned it. Steve said that Jason was fickle and when he was loved up, he didn't want to come out to play. By play, I assumed he meant for a few drinks and a laugh, watching the footie.

He came around and said he wasn't surprised that we'd split up. Steve had often had one-night stands and affairs over the years, almost on a weekly basis.

He would regularly bring women back to our home and have them in our marital bed. He was even seeing another family friend for on and off for a number of years. This family friend was single but knew me very well. I was embarrassed. This was news to me. I'd always thought he had been faithful. I'd never had concern or call to question his behaviour.

Jason said that there had been scores of girls and he recommended an STD test just make sure. I didn't mention the abortion and all the tests I'd had then.

"I stopped hanging about with him Elise, it was just getting a bit embarrassing and felt awful for you," he said trying to defend himself.

He said Steve had defended his actions to him by saying,

"Elise is the same. She works abroad, she goes up to Yorkshire, what do you think she's doing then?"

The truth was I was working or visiting family with Sophia. I was working hard for our new home, for our future. Working so hard I was too exhausted for anything, let alone an affair.

Another friend messaged a few months later to tell me the same things.

He revealed some detail about a family friend and their on/off relationship for a number of years and how it was getting really stupid as she'd threatened to tell me.

"Why didn't you tell me?" I said.

"Because you wouldn't have listened, and Steve would have silenced me and made me look a fool. You know what he's like."

"Actually, I'm not sure I do anymore," I said quietly trying to take it all in.

I was pleased Steve's so-called friends were all coming out in support for me; like my own cheerleading team except thirteen years too late.

There were tales of prostitutes and many of his trips away weren't entirely work related. I suspected he'd been escorting also but I couldn't prove it.

He'd been approached by a guy and asked to do some escorting just after I'd given birth to Sophia. He was considering it as a way of paying off the mortgage quickly.

I was disgusted he should even contemplate it I threw myself into work. If I earned good money, he wouldn't need to go out escorting other women.

Besides, what was wrong with him taking me out? His wife and the mother of his child?

I was starting to learn that the Steve I had married was not the person I thought he was. He was a liar. Every word and action had been pre-meditated, like a serial killer grooming his victims with every eloquent word. I never really knew him but nor did anyone else. His whole life had been a fabrication, a carefully controlled show and I had been Steve's puppet.

I felt disgusted and stupid.

In truth nothing surprised me anymore. I'd fallen in love with someone else, someone equally troubled although less manipulative. By this point I wasn't bothered anymore. Steve was a narcissist; I hadn't realised it until he left and his behaviour became more erratic. The more I ignored him, the worse his behaviour became. I was his toy to chew, kick, and run down. He wouldn't be happy until he'd succeeded.

Dealing with someone with a narcissistic personality is difficult on number of levels

140

First of all, narcissists are functioning psychopaths. They have no ability to love like the majority of the population but can make a plausible attempt at looking like they love and care.

- They can't see it. A lifetime of social conditioning and being told they are the most wonderful being on earth and can do no wrong. Low and behold anyone who questions this.

I remember Steve's Mum before her illness parading him around Tesco saying, *'look at my son isn't he beautiful, isn't he successful'*. He was 32 at the time.

She would do this regularly.

I found it weird. It was abuse, too incestuous and Oedipus complex for my liking.

He reassured me it was her way of loving him and said if I had Mum that loved me, I'd understand better. Personally, I thought it was creepy, telling the world your grown-up adult son was like God, a lie that had to be kept up throughout Steve's life.

Holidays were fun with Steve when the chilled out, easy going side of Steve came out to play. The pre-vacation rituals were tedious. He would take all his clothes to the ironing shop and when they returned pristine in polythene bags, he would lay them out on the bed putting them together in an array of outfits. Various hats (he was going bald and didn't want people to know), tops, trousers, and shoes were on display ready for him to try on. I would have to spend an hour telling him how he looked in each outfit and what he should wear on what day and with which holiday activity.

For example: white linen trousers with blue short sleeved shirt and pale grey hat would be great for a day sightseeing.

I can't believe I entertained such antics, but I loved him and was never going to get anyone better.

- With narcissists no matter what mistakes they make, someone else has to take the blame. They are master deflectors and skilled in on looking while others get into trouble.

- Crafty charmers. They can make a valid justification or plausible excuse for any situation. Because of this, those in responsible jobs such as solicitors, police, teachers are easily fooled.

- Narcissists are insecure individuals who seek to destroy others to make themselves look better.
A lifetime of poor parenting and being told you are a god-like wonder must take its toll. An act that is difficult to keep up. When people like me realise they are just a normal everyday person who makes mistakes it throws them off guard. I did this with Steve. He hated the fact I wasn't in awe of him anymore. The veil had come off and saw he was just the same as anyone.
He sought to make me appear neurotic and ridiculous. He would purposely create false situations so I'd retaliate, making him look like the better person. He created scenarios that made me look like an unfit parent and at one point convinced Sophia she'd better off living with him. This broke my heart and my mental state got worse.

- Narcissists attract either those they see as weak and easily controlled, or worst still, someone they see as successful so it can have prestige. Never be more successful than a narcissist or they will seek to break you. Jealousy creeps in. Steve spurred me on with his negativity, I was used to negative reinforcement and it made me try harder. Having been brought up by a jealous Mother, I was used to trying to be good at things just to please. I did this throughout my marriage.

-Narcissists have a sense of entitlement.
I remember one Valentine's Day; Steve had a meeting and convinced the business he was working for that I would be upset. Therefore, he suggested they pay for a hotel, dinner, and champagne for us.
Truth be known, I didn't care at all, it was just another day to me. This sense of entitlement manifested in all sorts of ways and when he didn't get his own way, he would manipulate a situation, so he did. Everyone danced to his tune. He was never angry, never raised his

voice, and could flirt between cold hard logic and emotional connection with ease.

I learnt to manage it, I didn't know until he left that I was destroyed, mentally broken. 13years of dealing with this man had drained me. The mask I'd worn for so long had come off, revealing a emotionally scarred woman.

My imminent divorce was causing all sorts of problems. Steve just wouldn't let go, he needed to have the upper hand and wanted to win. No one was winning, so he was hell bent on destroying me, so I'd back down.

Steve had paperwork to back up his arguments. He knew every trick in the book.

Sending me on wild goose chases for information in order to buy him time to hide information and money.

The theory, I suppose, was if he pulled on my emotional heart strings and had me trying to prove things the attention would be taken away from his misgivings.

The more I battled with him, the more he got his manipulative claws into Sophia. We were at deadlock but by getting into Sophia's head, he could get to me. He wanted me to chase him, to be in love with him, but that ship had long sailed. The tighter he held onto to breaking me the more detached I became. I used my imagination to escape the torture.

She would come to our house only to ask if she could go home, by 'go home' she meant to Steve's house.

For her, Steve's house was fun, there were kids to play with, she could be a child.

At our home, she saw me having a meltdown and flitting between being drunk and angry to sad and tearful. I was alone and Sophia was my only sanctuary, the only thing I had left.

Steve's lengthy e-mails on how to parent Sophia on topics such as 'how to make a healthy packed lunch' to 'how to dress her appropriately for a school outing'. As this type of stuff wasn't apparently my 'thing', he always felt the need to control me.

In the beginning he'd been charming and swept me off my feet. This continued at various points throughout our marriage. It was all lies and image. I now know he'd had multiple affairs, sometimes having numerous women in one night.

One Sunday night when Sophia was at Steve's, I was laying on my kitchen floor sobbing. I wanted my life to end, I couldn't get rid of the man, he just wouldn't leave me alone. Would I ever be rid of him? He made me resent Sophia, Sophia my little rock, my reason to stay alive. Without her I wouldn't have had a connection to Steve. He knew this and used it to his advantage.

I just needed someone to talk to, so I phoned Liam. He was the only one I trusted at this point. Having no friends in common or not knowing my family or Steve, he was a safe bet. I think I was the same for him too. As usual he was his cheery self.

"Hi Beaut, how are you?" I liked it when he called me Beaut, it made me feel attractive.

"I'm not good, found out more about Steve," I said tearfully said. "I'm so fucking sick of hearing shit about Steve, it's never ending," I screamed at him.

I imagined him pulling the phone away from his ear to avoid the shrill.

"He's a prick Els, why are you still letting him get to you? No one will want to go out with you while you are still giving that knob head air space," he said defending me.

What did he mean no one will want to go out with me? Did he mean that was why I'm single? Did he mean, *he* would go out with me if I stopped talking about him?

144

He'd never met Steve, but he hated him and he was venomous when he referred to him. I could detect him protecting me.

"Seriously Els, you're a strong bird, the guy's a fuckwit end of. So, stop even mentioning him because it pisses me off. Why can't you get on with your life, I just want to see you happy."

There was a hint of jealousy in Liam, almost like he didn't want me to have a past.
I think there was a jealous side to Liam, but it only endeared me more and I wasn't sure why. Maybe, I thought the jealous streak showed he cared.
Liam was a funny one, it took time and patience for him to open up. He did try a bit and I was flattered. I was sure no one else could talk to him like I could. He seemed to have a vulnerability about him – something stopping him from emotionally letting go and he saw me as easy to talk to. I was someone who didn't pass judgement.
I knew I had to be patient, like a Mother protecting it's wounded offspring. I wanted to help him and protect him. But most of the time he just wouldn't let me.
Two steps forward, five steps back. A glimmer of hope here and there in this constant cat and mouse game. There was the occasional surrender as he told me things but then held back, going back into his shell and ignoring me for weeks. I wasn't giving in; tenacity is in my blood, and being from Yorkshire we don't give up too easily.

This boy, he hated me calling him a boy, was hard work and I was determined to crack him.
Even if he didn't find me attractive and I'd been banished to the 'friend-zone' there was a loving connection there, almost unconditional. I was his friend, and that went beyond any sexual attraction.
He was an odd seesaw kind of character. On one hand he was inspirational, supportive, caring, and looked at me with doe eyes. On

145

the other hand, he was like a sledgehammer with me, ignoring me, cold, blunt, and elusive.

He had things to say, I was sure. To do a job which involves caring but to be so emotionally cut off didn't seem right. Why wouldn't he talk to me?

Why couldn't the stupid immature idiot see I wanted to help him? I tried every trick in the book. Self-disclosure, empathy, directness, it just didn't work.

I was just trying to help; help while dealing with my own crap.

I didn't have a me, a helper, someone to have my back and defend me against all the gossip and manipulation. The humiliation I faced at the school gates on a daily basis, someone who cared. I needed a 'me' more than he did. Instead I projected what I needed onto him in the hope he'd help, but he didn't, he didn't know how. I was the grown up and he was the child.

The problem with Liam was, because of his lack of flattery and attention, he became my verbal punchbag.

If I was having a bad day, I'd contact him and rant and cry. I'd get angry with him.

But he never budged, I would hit him in the face with my words but all the sound the noise just repelled off him, like oil on water, like that had happened to him so many times before, that he was numb to it. Occasionally he'd tell me to stop but his voice was so distant and weak, it was almost childlike and I couldn't hear it.

He let me rant and rave then he'd disappear for weeks. Leaving me to think. But not once did he offer to help! The bastard just let me sort it all out for myself.

And I'm so glad he did because I became strong, so stronger.

The frustrating idiot knew that, and that that's why he did it. Just like I knew his girlfriend wasn't right for him. I would often get drunk and tell him this.

146

"She's no good for you, she's manipulating you."

Then in fear of further rejection, I would follow up with;

"But neither am I, I'm no good for you."

I let him carry on and learn; knowing I'd be there when he needed me, like safety net. That's true love. Knowing that you can't be with someone but still being there for them.

He had it in him to love, he just didn't know how.

He brought out a different side in me, a patient, caring and nurturing side. One that had been latent throughout my marriage.

I wasn't even angry at him half the time; I was angry at myself for needing him.

Chapter 22
Arriving at the Orphanage

The coach pulled up at the station in Pokhara and I was surprisingly relaxed by the nine-hour journey, considering the coach nearly veered off the road several times throughout the trip.

I walked down the steps and scanned my surroundings, looking once again for a toilet.

I grabbed my backpack which was even heavier due to buying a couple of bits and pieces in Delhi. My favourite purchase was an applique style tablecloth with bright embroidered flowers. This was going to look wonderful on my dining room table.

I headed towards the toilet, which in usual Nepali style smelled terrible. Not wanting to put my backpack on the floor I attempted to pee while balancing it on my back, a difficult but interesting task and was relieved after the incident at the airport that I managed it.

I sat on a small white plastic chair outside a local bar in the mid-afternoon sun and waited to be collected.

I was waiting about 15 minutes, yet again, not really knowing where I was going or the logistics. Two local men were staring at me and one offered to give me a lift into town.

"Walking tours?" one man, a rather reedy toothless looking guy, enquired.

"No, I here for the Happy Home," I said

"Happy one?" said the toothless man. To be honest, teeth were a rarity over here. A full set of teeth was a lucrative as a roast chicken dinner. He looked puzzled and I was starting to think this place might not exist. After all, I hadn't met Asim, just been to his house. Maybe they'd brought me over as some aged whore ready to traffic for a specialist Nepali market.

I got up to grab a coke from the bar and just as I did, a cheeky boy of about ten or eleven rushed over to greet me.

"Elise?" he asked smiling at me with his impish grin.

"Yes?" I responded.

"I Anil," he announced.

"Well it's very nice to meet you Anil," I said emphasising *A-nil*, nodding at him and giving him eye contact to ensure I'd pronounced his name correctly. He nodded back and smiled, so I assumed it was correct. By his side was a somewhat weathered, sullen looking women who on further inspection was probably in her late 20's. She looked like she had the weight of the world on her painfully bony shoulders. I presumed this was Susila, the house mother.
I was expecting a more matriarchal figure than this, someone who oozed authority. But this woman looked like a wounded animal caught in a trap and didn't appear to be able to manage herself let alone an orphanage full of kids.
I asked A-nil if he could speak English.

"I no speak inglis well," he said in very broken language, to which Susila smiled and gave him a look.

I was worried, how the hell could I communicate only knowing two words in Nepali?

This was going to be a short-lived conversation, I thought.

He let out a belly laugh and said,

"Jisteko! I joke Mrs, we speak English all day at school," he said in perfect English.

149

He was going to be trouble, I could sense it, this kid had banter and cute charm, and anyone who knew my obsession with Liam would say I'm a sucker for that.

"Who is we? Do you have brothers and sisters, at home?" I enquired.

"Just brother," said Anil using the singular term when I knew he meant multiples, as it was an orphanage there had to be more than one child living there.

"How many? One? Two?" I said

"Seven," he thundered at the top of his voice and smiled. A big white cheeky perfect smile lighting up his face.

"Oh no! Seven boys!" I joked.

"Do you have children? Where is your husband?" Anil asked.

How very intrusive, I thought. Nepali people are about as subtle as a brick when it comes to asking personal questions. I avoided the husband question,

"I have a daughter, called Sophia, she's beautiful and intelligent and just like you she's very, very cheeky. Now I also have seven sons, I think," I said as I put my arms around him for a welcoming hug.

I clung onto that kid for dear life. I was missing Sophia and the hug was the best feeling in the world. He needed the hug too, he glowed with happiness for a tiny moment. This set the tone for the rest of the trip. Me and my boys! I thought, how wonderful.
A gaggle of boys and me, their mother. How proud I'd be looking after them. I usually told myself that I didn't like loads of kids, but I did, I loved kids. I didn't like spoilt western kids.

I didn't tolerate brats or bad behaviour, but I loved kids with character and cheekiness.

I arrived at the orphanage which was situated in a village in a valley about 3 miles from Lakeside, Pokhara. I was relieved this wasn't in the middle of the tourist bit as I'd come to get away from western civilisation and the town seemed full of walkers, although it was slightly out of season.

The orphanage was in a rural location with lots of green and brown patches of grass, obviously scorched by the afternoon rays. It was surrounded in the slight distance by the snow-capped mountains of the Annapurna range. Directly in front of the orphanage was a small broken road and beyond the road there was a river running through the valley, which I presumed eventually ended in Phewa lake, Lakeside.

Apart from villagers and the occasional cow, the area was remote, almost idyllic in its beauty but grounded in poverty. Here the boys were free roam around and play without fear of being run over. I would have loved Sophia to be somewhere like this, to feel free to roam.

The orphanage was a series of concrete buildings with congregated iron roofs, grey and dull with hard concrete dusty floors. On the back wall was a beautifully coloured mural of a tree with the title *'Happy Home'* displayed across it. There was a washing line hung between the buildings and on the line with navy blue school shirts and jumpers. This could easily have been a scene from the UK, but the grey stark buildings against a sunny mountainous backdrop kept my mind in Nepali reality.

On arrival I felt like Maria von Trapp, only there was house mother and seven boys, no captain waiting to greet me. I was told to act like their Mother, make them do their schoolwork, and abide by the local manners and customs of which I'd learnt the day before. I wasn't sure I remembered them all.

151

At this point in my life – post breakdown/meltdown/midlife illness - I'm not sure I was capable of looking after myself or even brushing my teeth, let alone being responsible for the boys.

"Mother! You're here! We have been waiting for you, we are so happy for you to share the Happy Home," called another boy; a beautiful looking, slim built boy of about fourteen or fifteen.

The boys picked me a flower from a nearby bush, which looked like some orange orchid. It omitted a red dye which they scraped across my forehead.

"It's called a Tikka spot," said one of the boys, a thin, sweet, smartly dressed child of eight or nine with charm and impeccable English.

I was overwhelmed by this ceremonial greeting but apprehensive. This place was like nowhere I'd ever experienced, it reminded me of a very small Victorian workhouse, reminiscent of Oliver Twist. It seemed cold and austere in decoration, but warm in heart. Hard and oppressive on first appearance but surrounded in love and respect. Within seconds a series of boys crowded around and just like a scene from the Sound of Music, they each said their name:

"Ridesh!"

"Samil!"

"Anil!"

"Tikka!"

"Ramesh!"

"Habir!"

"Kiran is not here," said the oldest boy, a tall gentlemanly looking teenager.

"His grandmother died, and he had to go to the countryside for her funeral," he carried on.

Half of me was confused the half disappointed. These aren't proper orphans, they have families, Grandparents. I was looking for kids with no family at all. Looking back, I'm disgusted with my view on this. Regardless of their family status these boys clearly needed help.
I was getting acquainted with my boys trying to say their names correctly. The Hindu names were easy although Ramesh and Ridesh were similar sounding and were bound to cause confusion. Some of the others were difficult to understand and I called Samil, Sammy for about a week until I saw it written in English.
I was busily hugging and greeting the boys when a sandy coloured mongrel bounded through the garden to greet me.

"This is Sheru, he's our dog!" said Ridesh.
*"He's **my** dog,"* argued Anil.

This was a very playful dog; he was definitely a mixed breed. A bit like a Labrador mixed with Japanese Akita, not to mention another four or five breeds, all unidentifiable.
Sheru appeared to be more of a handful than the kids. Sheru was yappy, playful, and bigger than the two younger boys with a cute black wet nose. He didn't really belong to the boys, but they'd officially adopted him. He actually lived down the road with another family but clearly preferred the boy's company better, and who could blame him. So, there I was in the middle of a remote Nepali village with my adopted sons' and their adopted dog Sheru, feeling quite bewildered. Just after my arrival, the boys had received a box of clothes, and just like a bunch of flesh grabbing vultures at a local car boot sale they were in the box trying on items. They were throwing the clothes around without any regard. They stripped off not caring about being naked in front of a stranger.

Clothes were strewn across the bare concrete floor of the living room, like they didn't understand the value of things. I'd expected children with nothing to have more respect for new things, but the truth was everything in their lives had been disposable up to this point and so were the clothes.

Tika, the oldest boy and man of the home, stepped in to help sort them into sizes.

"Samil, this one for you because it's the smallest," he said in English.

All the boys spoke in English around me, it made me feel special. They didn't need to; they could have chosen to alienate me and speak Nepali. As an elder – and I was practically ancient to them – they had intrinsic respect for me. I hadn't commanded it; they just projected this status onto me. Little did they know that I was a total and utter out of work failure who could barely get out of bed in the morning to comb my hair, but they needn't know that.

Habir had been donated a brand-new, beautiful, mint coloured, lightweight Benetton jacket. He paraded around the room showing it off, whilst his nose had colour matching trail of snot. How very avant-garde, a nice shade of mint green phlegm to match his new jacket. The poor kid appeared to have a terrible cold and no tissues. I suppose if he used his sleeve the colours would blend.

Within minutes of putting on the coat Habir ran over the road and into the field to play with Sheru. He was tugging at the poor dog's tail and play fighting. Sheru, being an excitable pup, tore the sleeve of the new jacket clean off, all whilst dragging Habir with his teeth.

Habir laid giggling on the floor leaving a trail of green fabric and even more green snot behind him.

At this moment I realised these boys and their dog were going to keep me on my toes.

Later that first evening we Face-Timed Sophia. Her pudgy little face popped up on the screen.

"Hi Mommy," she called almost welling up with tears. *"Mommy are you safe?"* she enquired.

"Yes sweetie, I'm safe. There's a few people who want to meet you," I said holding the phone so the boys could stare into it.

"Hi sister!" called the boys. I loved that they called her sister.

Sophia was overwhelmed by this gaggle of cheeky boys crowding around my tiny phone, all keen to meet her and say thank you for letting them have her Mummy for a few weeks.
I smiled, looking back at my little pudgy girl talking to the boys and I was proud.
The boys never asked to call me Mother, they just did. I melted, already proud of all of them all.

Chapter 23
Unhinged and Unloved

I felt like I'd been sucked up in a whirlwind of destruction and spat out again in a foreign land; disoriented and unsure of my surroundings. I trusted no one. My beautiful little girl was being turned against me, my neighbours were spying on me, who the hell was I to trust anymore?

I lived in the town Steve had grown up in and it had been a while since he left. Nothing had changed for the better and my life was spiralling out of control. I was drinking a lot and hanging around with drinkers.

He'd somehow managed to convince everyone that I was at fault and that I'd caused the divorce as he flicked between playing the victim and persecutor.

The story he told was of a poor depressed man with a heartless wife who just wanted to work. We had made a mutual decision. We just weren't getting on and I was becoming neurotic. What he failed to mention was how he'd slept with half of the town while I worked away and how he'd manipulated every situation to look good. It finally ended with him shagging and shacking up with the school cleaner.

I joked he was a pre-programmed robot, there wasn't a single action or word that he spoke that hadn't been meticulously thought out. Steve's speech moved as slowly as a chess master, planning his next move.

My rose-tinted glasses – the ones created by Steve I hasten to add – had come off, and what I now saw before me was a fraud. A weak man who had embellished his whole life to make him appear far more successful and confident than he actually was.

Steve always got his own way. He had a way of making people feel inferior to him, so no one ever felt intelligent enough to stand up to him. Except, just like the little boy in the emperor's new clothes, only I could see it. I was screaming for everyone else to see what I could, but no one was listening.

He'd let his guard down on a couple of occasions one where he pushed me out of the door and onto the ground, cutting my leg. He disliked that I didn't look at him in adoration like he was some God anymore. He was a normal guy to me, a normal guy with an inflated ego.

After a year apart he still believed I was madly in love with him. I wasn't.

The truth was I was madly in love with a cheeky junior Doctor who was more grounded than him, who wasn't flash or a boaster. With similar charm and pride but a bit insecure and unsure of himself, a worrier but real and non-judgmental. I didn't need fancy dinners and boasting about the things I'd done and seen. I didn't need all-inclusive holidays and designer labels.

I wanted fun and for most of the time, Liam made me laugh. He'd never met anyone like me, and I felt I intrigued him. He couldn't work me out, but I couldn't work him out either which was equally enticing. I was spellbound by him and he was a bit scared and intrigued by me. I had been erratic and moody in recent months and my personal life seemed to represent a middle class Jeremy Kyle show.

I flittered between feelings of high euphoria and extreme melancholy. I was starting to become more spiritual and meditating and trying to 'be' rather than 'do'.

Occasionally when reality hit so did feelings of isolation. I could no longer relate to people around me and even less than I had before. The only person who did seem to understand me was too evasive and immature to help. Too busy ignoring his own problems and distracting himself with work.

I opened the bottle of pink gin and poured myself a large measure. I salivated at its contents emptying into my glass, just the thought of its bitter rosiness hitting my taste buds was enough to get my mouth juices flowing. I went to the fridge and found a half full bottle of tonic. I carefully unscrewed the cap to avoid it fizzing everywhere.

I sat down on the sofa in silence; no T.V., no music, no laptop, no internet. Except I wasn't in silence; my mind was whizzing. My thoughts were noisy, and I couldn't control the din in my head.

'You've been a long time single, you can't get beyond a date, you fat useless, alcohol induced mess!' the voice in my head called out.

'You obsess about everyone you meet, what is wrong with you, you stupid middle-aged cow!' It continued.

I swallowed down a large measure of gin, then another, then another, then a fourth and final gulp until my glass was empty.

I text my dad;

"Hey Dad, how are you?"

No reply.

I text my Daughter;

"Hey Baby, how are you? Mummy is missing you like mad."

No reply.

It was 1am Sunday morning and both would be in bed. Consoling myself, I poured and even bigger glass of gin reducing the bottle to almost half. This time I drank it down like an athlete drinking water post marathon. A warm comfortable feeling wafted across my body. I text some more, this time one of my online dates. No answer. I posted some childhood pictures of Facebook with the caption, *'Hey, wasn't I cute?'*. No answer, not even a like.

I craved attention and going on Facebook stopped me texting Liam. I downed my drink and went and poured another. The warm feeling had subsided, and the loneliness came back, my head whirred.

I text Liam, no answer.

WhatsApp pinged;

"Hi sexy!" And a couple of dick pics from one of my online dates.
"Now you send me a sexy pic."

By sexy pic he meant *'Show me your tits!'*. Not quite drunk enough to
engage in this type of behaviour I ignored him.
I sent another message to Liam as an anecdote to this unsavoury
activity.

"Do you find me sexy or scary?" I wrote, knowing full well he'd never
respond to such a ridiculous message.
I wasn't actually trying to achieve anything other than a reaction. A
reaction meant contact and any form of contact was better than being
ignored.
He was online, he'd been online most of the evening. He was rarely
offline. I avoided looking at his Facebook page, this was childish and
stalkerish and under more sober situations and I disliked that type of
behaviour.
I went into the kitchen and poured another drink. I wasn't enjoying
the taste of gin anymore; I was very drunk and three quarters of the
bottle had disappeared down my throat.
I messaged Liam again in another unsuccessful attempt to get his
attention:

"I think I'm an alcoholic Liam, what do you think?"

I knew I wasn't an alcoholic, I was an attention seeking woman who
was depressed.
Still nothing from him. I wanted to scream. He'd opened my
messages. I wanted to smash the phone in frustration.
I staggered upstairs and into my room. I opened my underwear
drawer, almost pulling the small unit over in my drunken state. I
pulled out some underwear, my beautiful bright green bra and pants
that I'd bought from John Lewis in hope someone would eventually

get to see them. I put them on almost falling over as I stood on one leg. I examined myself in the mirror, my bum looked small and my boobs looked pert. I had consumed almost an entire bottle of gin, of course I looked hot, beer goggle hot!

I took a picture pouting in my underwear, half beautiful, half tragic, as my eyes turned in from excess alcohol consumption.

"Wanna Facetime?" I sent.

"Hell yeah, you're beautiful." my online date text back.
"You look amazing for your age." he put.

What did that even mean? Either I looked amazing or I didn't, what had age got to do with it

Within seconds I was talking filth on Facetime to a guy I'd never met while pissed up on gin. I oozed desperation, but in the few minutes it took to satisfy each other I felt loved and important. For a short time, I got what I wanted if not who I wanted.

My feelings of satisfaction subsided, and I messaged Liam.

"Is it wrong that I want to smash your face in?" I typed aggressively.

This time my ploy worked, and he did respond.

"Have you been drinking Els? And yes, to answer your previous question, I do think you have a drink problem." he carried on.

"Nah, I'm sober but just thinking what an absolute arsehole you are." I typed misspelling most of the words and peppering the text with inappropriate emojis. Overusing consonants so the text resembled a Welsh history book.

"I'm not replying to you when you are drunk, I don't like it." he replied.

160

"Why won't you ever pick up the phone and actually talk to me? I fucking hate you! My life was brilliant before I met you and now it's shit!"
"See what you're missing?" I sent him a picture of me in my underwear.

He replied,

"Els please don't send me stuff like that, I don't like it, it's not really you, you're not a tart so please stop acting like one."
"Els, you're a bright woman, you're funny, you're amazing and you're my mate."

He didn't say I was attractive though. I was never happy, and the guy couldn't win with me. Even if he had any feelings they would have disappeared after this mindless rampage.

"Go to bed and sleep it off and I'll call you tomorrow. I can't reason with you when you are like this."

Not content with his response I phoned him and screamed,

"Why won't you talk to me? Why do you ignore me? You're a cunt just like Steve! A womanising, non-committal cunt!"

He hung up and turned off his phone.

Chapter 24
Getting to Know the Boys

Customs and manners in Nepal were very different to those of your average Yorkshire lass. I know we can be primitive up North, but some of Nepali customs even made me baulk.

Firstly, there's the left and right-hand etiquette which is customary across Africa, Asia, and the Middle East.

Left hands are for toilet wiping, and right sides are for mixing and eating food. No matter how sloppy and wet either practice is, that is the purpose of those hands and neither of them should be mixed up. However, the younger boys not having a parental influence would often forget this practice, and I was there to guide, instruct and tell them when they got it wrong.

'Thank god I brought the toilet roll and my own spoon' was all I could think.

There was very little hot water available which made this even more interesting. But what the hell. *What was a bit of dysentery between friends and family?'* I thought as I looked at longingly my Imodium tablets, knowing we'd be acquainted sooner or later.

During the first days I spent with the boys I played football and table tennis. Not being a natural sportsperson, well one can't be good at everything, I was terrible. I certainly wasn't going to get a call to join the Olympic team in a hurry.

In the evening I stuck to what I was good at. Acting!

I read them 'The Tinderbox' by Hans Cristian Andersson, putting on my best character voices. I remembered as a child having the audiobook on a tape which I played over and over again, mastering the witch's voice, so I recreated it for the boys, my witchy voice rasping and gargling as I'd done as a 10 year old girl. The trip so far seemed to be about reliving my youth and getting back to the original me. My *'shoes off self'* as the psychologist Karl Jung would say.

One thing I've learnt over the years is that regardless of whether or not people understand a language, an animated voice and a funny face breaks down all cultural barriers and helps to understand. The kids were in stitches laughing at my oscar winning performance. Apparently, I'm a great witch! I secretly I enjoyed the book more than the boys. The worries of home and a looming court case disappearing with every chuckle.

When I'd finished, I went back to my bedroom and sat only my bed. I read through a note I'd written for Sophia. This wasn't a note for now, but one for my baby when she reached her teenage years and was able to understand the enormity of the situation.
I read back through the letter:

'My Dear Darling Sophia,

It is November 2017. You are 8 years old and I'm in bed trying to keep warm. You are having your dinner in the playroom and watching TV.
By the time you read this you'll be a teenager and hopefully will understand my words.
I'm so sorry for the last two years, for being a distant mom, but I haven't felt a lot of joy for a long time now. Since your Daddy left things have got worse for me. He has made my life hell and intentionally done it. Some of the strange things I do won't make sense to an 8-year-old but hopefully do to the young beautiful woman I know you will become.
At the moment, I am penniless and exhausted, and you have probably now discovered for yourself what type of man your Father is, as I will only give you this letter on discovery of his true behaviours. I tried to protect you from everything he has done and let you see him whenever you wanted to, usually half of the week. This hurt me, but I'm not a bad person so thought it was for the best for you.
Christmas is looming and I have no way of paying for anything. I really wanted what I think will be your last Santa Claus Christmas to be extra special. In truth I can't even afford to fix the boiler.

I love you more than anything in the world and I hope by the time you read this we are a happy family once again you, me, and if someone special comes into my life, them too.

There have been times when I've wanted to end it all and in truth, without you, my little ray of sunshine, I probably would have.

You are an amazing little girl (young woman now). I'm so proud of you.

You are my reason for living.

I don't have you Christmas Day again as you wanted to be with Daddy. It breaks my heart, but I understand. We will have the best Christmas Eve together snuggling up and watching movies and a big lunch.

I am so very scared of losing you and that your Daddy will want to take you permanently. I'm a good Mummy and I can't bear this thought. I think I've tried to tell you this without scaring you, but I'm scared too. I have no energy or money to fight a custody battle and a divorce. I will do what I can by any means to keep my baby girl, even if we are homeless.

You are my life, my reason for being, and I want you to grow up to be a happy, successful woman. Success is not about money but about how much you use the talents you have and make the best of them while still being happy.

Don't make the mistakes I did and even if you do, I'll be by your side supporting you. I'll always be here for you as you have been for me, my Little Rock and my earth angel.

Love you lots like jelly tots,

Mummy xxx'

The real meaning of my trip was starting to unravel, and I felt useful for the first time in ages. Street kids in Nepal don't get the opportunities these kids have, an education, play, and most of all me! My confidence was coming back.

xxxxx

Chapter 25
Inspiration

My life felt out of control and Steve was punishing me for not pining for him. He wanted me to still want him, it made him feel special and massaged his ego, an ego that was starting to falter. I didn't want him anymore and our fun times were a distant memory looked at through sepia lens.

His new partner was normal, she'd never been out with a narcissist before so didn't understand how to manage the situation. Once I'd gotten over him and realised what he was like, I felt sorry for her. Like me, she'd been sold a dream, but unlike me she didn't have the strength to get out of it.

They argued because she was used to being in a normal relationship, she didn't know the rules of dealing with a sociopath. He needed to be managed by his rules, end of. Don't argue, don't fight, and don't disagree or you will look like the idiot.

I was watching it happen in slow motion like a weird movie.

I'd shed my old self like a snake shedding its skin.

But I was anxious my new skin wouldn't grow. It didn't seem to be emerging and as a result I was left personality-less with nothing but a void. Who the hell was I? The feeling was strange. I just wanted to disappear without a trace. I didn't want to be at home, I didn't want to be at work, I didn't want to go out. Being with Dad or any family left me cold, I didn't want to go on holiday. I didn't want to be anywhere.

I was transitioning into a new person but couldn't see it.

The old 'me' was cocky, a tad materialistic but despite this I always cared. I helped people and I like doing that.

I was nothing. A drained worn out nothing with nothing more to give. People – the wrong people – had taken my soul, they'd had the best of me and still expected more, and I was ready to give up. I had given up, I just wanted to stay in bed and cry.

Steve had had my energy, Liam had taken my energy, Sophia, work, friends, and there was no more Elise left give. My cup was empty, and it needed filling up but how was I going to fill it up again?

Liam eventually came around again, this time for a short visit and a cup of coffee on his way biking in the nearby the forest. He'd cancelled previously because his girlfriend didn't like him seeing other women and I couldn't really blame her. He wasn't exactly the most faithful and reliable person. I think I'd refer to him as an opportunist and being cute there was always opportunity.

Except it was different with me, he had plenty of opportunity with me, but I was sex repellent and he no longer saw me as an object of fancy. I'd been well and truly banished to the 'friendzone'. I was his buddy, his mentor, his agony aunt, and after that first occasion when he was single, we never engaged in sex again, just banter, laughs and the occasional disagreement.

Short visits always lead to big conversations with him. This time following the revelations about my ex I told him how depressed I was and that I wanted out, out of the country and out of life. I was ready to give it all up. I contemplated what it would be like if I just left without a trace. I thought about the mechanics of suicide and even admitted to him that I had bought the tablets from several chemists and a large bottle of gin. I was serious about the plan, but not brave enough to do it.

I don't know why people say it's the coward's way out, it's not. Suicide is serious and it takes a very ill and very brave decision. For me, I knew mine was temporary, and intrinsically I knew Liam had been brought into my life for a reason. I needed to find out what that reason was, I couldn't die yet. My poor Sophia would be scarred for life, I'd never put her through such horrible pain. She was already suffering as a result of the split.

166

I think Liam was a bit worried about me still not working and getting a bit down. He always seems to turn up when I'm on the brink of depression or about to do something drastic.

"I need to find you something to do, something that will bring back your spark," Liam said hurriedly, like he was desperately trying to not talk about my depression.

"You need to do nothing, you need to sort your own shit out mate, not mine!" I snapped at him. I was starting get short with him.
"You've never seen my spark only me in this state. You've only ever known me single that's why we met in the first place - remember? You shagged me in hotel room then ran away and got a girlfriend," I continued snapping at him.
"I hate you and I want to smash your face in, you're like the rest of them," I ranted.

"Erm, I think you'll find you ignored me for 6 months, you Dingbat," he said.

He was right, I did. In the meantime, he'd found himself a girlfriend and was clearly very distracted by her.

"Well I didn't want to date a player, a tart. I prefer my men a bit more faithful than you!" I shouted back.

"What? like your ex-husband? Would you prefer I was like him?" he howled back in jealousy.

"How fucking dare you! Get out of my house, you horrible bastard, just fucking leave!" I screeched.

Not used to seeing me in this state. He sat back in shock and aiming to calm me down, he hurriedly blurted out;

What do you like doing? You like the theatre, don't you?"

"But I hate theatre people, they're weird," I sulked like five-year-old.

"Well you're a bit weird too, ain't ya?" he joked with a glint in his eye in an unsuccessful attempt to calm me down. He was trying a bit too hard and it wasn't working.

"Yes, well I don't want to hang about with other weirdos, do I?" I barked again.

He stared at me with those long lashes and beautiful piercing green eyes.

"Don't look at me like that, you womanising idiot, I won't fall for it."

I looked at him closely he was watching my every movement like a shark circling his prey. I melted.

"Well apart from you, you're my fave weirdo," I said raising an eyebrow and flirting with him.

My heart felt like it was going to burst and as I longingly looked into his eyes. He knew exactly what he was doing. How many times had he played this game? How many women had looked in those eyes and melted, like I had?
I wasn't the only woman who felt like this with him, all women flirted with him. He was cheeky and this was part of the act.
Everyone fancied him and that was the problem. Why would he go out with a washed-up older woman with a child when he could have a pert twenty something or even better, several pert twenty somethings? But no one saw his vulnerable side, his self-deprecation, and his feelings of unworthiness. He could hide that by flirting with a young girl. Not with me, I unnerved him, and I would say things like;

168

Come on Liam, you're better than that, stop playing me, I'm not falling for your flirting."

Or I'd look at him with a smirk and he'd say

"You think I'm bullshitting you, don't you? I'm not. I can never lie to you; nothing gets past you."

He was right. I knew when I was being played by him. He couldn't help himself, he'd done it for so long and he never trusted anyone, so it was his default defending position. I knew his game, lay on the cheekiness with wink and a smile and get away with murder.

I was still reeling over what to do and hoping he'd give me an answer.

He downed his cup of coffee and stood up and walked towards me, gave me a massive squeezy hug, gently kissed my cheek, and headed towards the door to leave.

"Well you'll figure something out Bab, it'll just come to you," he said nonchalantly in his Brummie accent.

There again with his vague statements, which somehow seem to work on me.
I think he knows I'm stubborn and whatever he or anyone suggests I'll do the absolute bloody opposite. He knows this because he's the same, like personality twins.
I paced up and down my kitchen with the occasional huff and puff for about ten minutes, thinking over things. I'll show him! If he can't give me ideas the little prick, I'll get my own ideas!!
Before finally saying;

"I think I'd really like to work in an African village helping the kids."

"Well do it!" he said. "Stop bloody moaning about life and do it!"

169

"I can't, I've got to think of Sophia, I'm a Mum. I can't leave her. What will people think? What will they say?"

"Who cares about them Els, who are they anyway?"

With a wink and a smile and a gentle friendly tap on my shoulder he said,

"You'll make it work I know you will."

Those eyes were amazingly hazel but changed colour to a sparkling emerald when they caught the light. I felt myself feel warm inside and once again my heart fluttered.
He had an Irish look about him, I think he had Irish family. He had mimicked a brilliant accent on the first night I met him, such a bloody joker. He was the only guy who had made me smile in eighteen months, but he was complicated and sure to break my heart.
He left and I wasn't sure if I was ever going to see him again. No plans had been made and he seemed very loved up with his pretty young girlfriend. Who knows? He never made plans. I admired his laid-back attitude, his spontaneity thrilled me.
It also frustrated the hell of me filled me full of doubt.

He went and I was left with a ton of questions, no answers or solutions. I was trying to figure it out for myself. I was always left figuring things out for myself. He'd throw in a suggestion like a hand grenade and I'd be left to pick the pieces and make sense of it.
I sat for about an hour contemplating what he said. I opened my Macbook started to look at volunteering projects.

There were hundreds:

- India
- Morocco
- Thailand

170

- Ecuador
- Bolivia
- China
- NEPAL!

I'd always fancied Nepal and wanted to see Everest. There I was, reeling from our conversation on the MacBook looking at projects in Nepal. I looked at all sorts of things; teaching, animal projects, health projects.
Steve had talked about going to Nepal and the bitch in me thought he'll never go with too many mouths to feed and a boring new girlfriend, but I will!
Two days later I sent Liam a message.

"Hi Gorgeous! I'm off to Nepal Christmas Day to work in an orphanage."

I could see he was online, and he responded immediately.

'WTF - where did that come from?" he sent back.

"You!" I messaged back with a winky emoji face.

"I never told you to go to Nepal! I'm not even sure I know where it is. How long for? Can I come?"

"You didn't need to, and no you can't come I'm going to find myself and get away from you, you unreliable arsehole." I blew a kiss, which is very unlike me.

He'd already rejected me at this point. I was too proud to admit I was doing it to impress him and piss Steve off a tad.
Liam and I had a strange relationship. I barely knew him but knew him so well.

He'd pop up when I thought life couldn't get worse, he'd re-adjust my mind set and off I'd go on my next adventure or trying out my next idea. I always felt refreshed after his visit or messages.

At times I felt like his mother telling him off, other times I was his mentor and teacher, guiding him, offering career advice, and then sometimes his mate, providing the laughs and stupidity. Very occasionally I was a source of passion and lust as he pursed his his lips and examined my body with his eyes, not daring to touch it for fear of doing something wrong. I wanted him to, I really wanted him to do that.

The week leading up to my trip, everything had taken a turn for the worse. My Grandmother who had been in a care home for many years died. I was sad that another part of my childhood had gone. We'd been very close when I was young and a younger woman, and I will always remember her as kind, caring, and trying to keep the peace between my Mum and her Sister.

Family feuds meant I hadn't seen that side of the family for years, so felt a bit bad grieving too much, but I did. I wept for a piece of my childhood that had gone.

Two days before I left, Steve's baby arrived, another little girl. Sophia was over the moon and I had to endure endless photos and excitement while planning for Christmas and my trip.

"Mummy look at my baby sister, she's beautiful isn't she?" she proudly showed me.

"Yes sweetie, she's a darling." I replied, emotionless.

I was so glad I'd booked to go away, it meant Sophia could spend time with her new sister without my negativity. I was still dead inside, and this wasn't the time to be like this.

It was a happy time for her, and I wanted her to enjoy it, with her Dad and his new family.

Chapter 26
Parents Day and a Cool Concert

It was Parents' Day at school and my day started at 6 am. There was a mist over the mountain in front, it was 3 degrees, and I was like an icicle.

The boys got up and put their playing clothes on and we had a table tennis match. I was hopeless at table tennis and kept hitting the ball too hard, flinging it into a nearby garden.

I helped Susila make breakfast of Daal Baat. This time with soya beans, potatoes, and lentils.

Daal Baat - rice and lentils for every meal. I thought Yubaraj was joking when he'd said that every meal was this, I'd seriously hoped he was. But it was only for a short time, so I dealt with it and was thankful for what I got.

Seriously I don't know why the Z list celebs moan about it on 'I'm a Celebrity'. I got used to it and liked the fact it was healthy. Lukewarm water and Daal Baat was a welcome change to eating rubbish and getting fat over Christmas. I knew I was going to lose weight this festive season, bonus! Steve could shove his 'fat simpleton' text up his arse I thought.

I talked to Susila about her late husband and was intrigued by how he died so young. He got ill, and they had no money for medicine. He died about four years ago when she was 24. The way she described his death made it sound like cancer or some sort of progressive illness. I didn't get the indication he died suddenly.

Her English wasn't very good an knew no Hindi, so I pieced her story together by using an English dictionary and by the limited existing vocabulary she knew. Her understanding was better than her speech. She had been brought to the 'Happy Home' with her small son Ridesh two years before, to look after the boys. At least it meant Ridesh had a home and was surrounded by a band of brothers.

I swept and mopped the floors then helped the younger boys get ready for school. It was an important day for the boys and also in a strange way it was important for me.

It was New Year's day 2018, and while my friends back home were nursing hangovers, I was playing Mary Poppins at school, a role I relished in. I wore make-up, nothing over the top, but enough to look respectable should I be introduced to the boys' teachers. People weren't rich here, but I detected a visit to school would ensure the parents wore their best clothing. Values were old fashioned and official engagements such as temple and school were important.

I wore my fuchsia cotton top with black walking leggings and my boots, and placed Sophia's girly headband in my hair, wearing it made me feel closer to her.

I felt feminine for a change. I'd traded my Louboutin's in for walking boots and my little black dress for lycra leggings. I wasn't in Nepal to look glamorous or go on the pull, I was there to help. Besides I couldn't pull in a room full of desperate men in the U.K. – let alone in rural Nepal.

Parents day was supposed to be fun for the boys, it's a day of no schoolwork and they get to perform a dance or mess about. Guess which my boys did? Yep, no dancing or sitting still for them. In, fact I haven't got a clue where half of them were on that day.

We arrived at school, and it was busy, really, really busy. Back home I would have panicked at not finding Sophia amongst a sea of faces. Here I knew my boys were tough and independent so no need to worry.

There was easily over 1,500 kids at that school. Usually all penned in their miserable dark looking classrooms.

Except today, Parents Day, they were let loose like animals in open cages. They were wild, running around like lunatics and no one seemed to be supervising. Supervising? Was that a western thing? Safeguarding and chaperoning just didn't exist in Nepal.

I sat quietly in a chair on the front row and was accosted by about a dozen nine - twelve-year-old girls. I showed them pictures of Sophia, and they said she was 'soooo pretty'.
They said,

"You are pretty, we like your hair!" They should see brushed and straightened.
"We love your nails!" They're actually false and looking a little bit infected under the skin.

"We want your face!" Yeah, it looks better with more makeup on.

I wanted to take those girls home with me, bless them. They were far more complimentary than any of the boys in my life, orphans or the adult ones.

I sat and sat and sat for two hours, and nothing happened. I was bored and restless, which is not a surprise. I can't watch thirty minutes of T.V. without getting bored. Back home I can't watch normal cinema. I have to go to the 4D showings to be thrown around and have water and air squirted in my eyes, anything less and I fall asleep. So, decided to take a walk to the lake. Forty-five minutes later I sat and had a coffee. I met a man and his nephew from Derby and chatted a while before walking back to the school.
I arrived back at school to find out Samil had danced and I'd missed it.

"Did you see him Mother?" Ridesh had said. I wanted the ground to swallow me up. Do I lie and say it was wonderful? No, I'll be honest I thought.

"No, Sweetheart I missed it, I had to go somewhere." I said really ashamed particularly as 'somewhere' had been a cafe and nowhere important. Damn my stupid impatience!

I could hear Ridesh translating to his brother Samil that Mother had missed his dance.

I saw the look on his little face, one of disappointment. I was gutted and felt like a terrible Mother once again. There's nothing like missing a kid's school play, sports day, or dance recital to make you feel like the worse parent on earth.

I remembered this when I almost didn't attend Sophia's first violin concert.

Feeling embarrassed and like I had to make it up to the boys, I sat and watched the rest of the show with them; well the ones who would sit still long enough – mainly Ridesh, and Ramesh, and Samil. Other parents tried to converse with me, but as my Nepali stretched as far as Namaste and Jiskeko, the chat was limited. I resorted to smiling and gesturing.

The school handed out samosas, and I spent most of the time telling Samil not to eat with his left hand. The parents seemed very impressed that I was teaching the boys manners. Nodding at me attentively.

I thoroughly enjoyed the dancing. I loved the colourful traditional Nepali costumes jingling along. Although I've got to admit after three or four dances it all appeared to look the same. Cleary I was a discerning critic.

I wondered off again to look at the science projects of the older children. There was an array of inventions and mechanical human body parts with explanations written at the side, all in English. The children gave me an explanation of the workings each in perfect English and I sat there in awe.

"Hey! Auntie, come look at my project," said one boy.

"No Auntie look at mine, mine is an ecological system, see how the water flows Auntie?" shouted another boy.

"Auntie, you don't want to look at the boy's boring project, look at this one. It's a girl's one," said one proud girl showing off her model of the digestive system complete with English labels.

Auntie was the respectful term all women of a certain age were referred to and I found it strange. I have nieces and a nephew, but they never call me Auntie.

The onlooking teachers looking proud that they could finally test out their education on a real-life English person.

After a few hours and a look around each boys' classroom and a chat with their teachers, the small boys and I left and went for a walk down the river. I liked the river; it was peaceful and gave me lots of thinking time. I could skim stones with the boys and keep life simple.

It's difficult trying to please several boys aged seven to sixteen. The little ones want to play, and the big ones want music. I decided to spend the non-school days with the little ones and evenings with the big ones.

I'd promised to take Tika to the festival because his favourite singer was headlining.

I really couldn't be bothered at 6pm. I was cold and tired and didn't fancy the 90-minute walk into town. I had three hours to wait until we were going, and I knew it was going to be a night of Nepali rap and pop music. Rap has to be my least favourite music with grime becoming a close second.

I didn't want to let Tika down; I could see his disappointed face as I tried to explain I was too tired to do anything.

Being easily swayed and not wanting to upset the poor kid, off I went into town to the concert.

"There's a shorter way, I know, it only takes about forty-five minutes," said Tika.

We took a so-called shortcut over through the slums. I wobbled across rickety bridges and ledges with water beneath. It was dark and only the moon lit our way. I was actually quite scared thinking; one wrong footing and I'd be in the cold icy water and swept upstream into the lake.

I would never do this back home. Back home even for a gig, I'd have a full face of make-up on, my skinny jeans, and some form of heeled boot.

Here I was naked faced, in my gym leggings, hoody, and a pair of hiking boots.

I did manage to put some lipstick on. I'd rather be naked than not wear my new trademark red lipstick.

We got to the concert; it was heaving with Nepali teenagers. I couldn't think of anywhere I'd rather not be, than there. It was freezing and colder than the night before when I'd attended the same venue with Ramesh, I was so tired but Tika's face lit up, and that made it all worthwhile. He watched the singers and dancers in admiration. I like watching and dancing, although I am theatrical, I'm a terrible dancer myself.

The build-up to Low-Ri was excellent, the presenters, the other singers, all in anticipation of this god like rapper.

9pm arrived, and the crowd went crazy;

"Low-Ri, Low-Ri, Low-Ri, LOW RI, YEAH!" the crowd chanted in staccato type rhythm.

Then, half of the teenage population of Nepal's idol arrived on stage.

"YEAHHH! We love you, Low-Ri!" shouted the girls next to me.

Just the like the revealing of the Wizard in the Wizard of Oz, it was an anti-climax, as the 5ft 5 midget Nepali rapper bounced around the stage like a five-year-old on smarties. The only thing I liked was that he sang in English, thank goodness!

With a sense of relief, we left as soon as Low-Ri had finished. Tika thought it was a cool night, and said;

"Thank you, cool Mother, for taking me!"

178

We took a taxi back – I wasn't in the mood for that walk again. I was determined to do something we could all enjoy tomorrow.

Chapter 27
Boating and Chips

The day after the concert the boys were off school again, another holiday day. There appeared to be a few a month and I wasn't sure if they were just pulling my leg or not as the other kids in the village seemed to be at school. I was told that they apparently went to another school.

I think secretly they wanted to spend the day with me playing by the river, and who could blame them, it was idyllic. I was happy to have the boys around as it got me out of gardening. They were fun and interesting and taught me a lot about parenting boys.

I had a girl and she was very happy to play alone and entertain herself, she was sociable but didn't need constant stimulation.

The boys needed activity, they had a lot of energy and needed to let off steam. Sitting reading a book or making up stories, as Sophia would do, wouldn't have been enough to keep them alert.

They wanted football games, fishing, rowing, and running up and down hills. I loved it but they exhausted me. My body was slowly recovering from a mental breakdown, so it wasn't quite as energetic as it used to be.

We started the day washing clothes in a bowl outside. I scrubbed mine with a stone and a bar of soap. My stuff didn't seem to get clean. The white t-shirt I'd bought for my trip was now grey with a hint of yellow. The water was ice cold. It had been warm in the daytime and I got hot, so the smell of sweat clung to my clothes like stale onion soup. My new perfume; *'Perspiration with a hint of solvent'*, it was the perfect aroma for the white-collar hippy I was gradually morphing into. I secretly enjoyed being stinky and dirty, it reminded me of a happy childhood memories rolling in mud and making soil pies in my Grandad's back garden. Despite the corporate garb I was used to wearing, I was a dirty girl at heart. Steve wouldn't allow me to be scruffy, it wasn't good for his reputation.

"Back in England we have washing machines," I said attempting to educate them.

"We know mother!" said Anil curling his nose as if I was treating them like uneducated barbarians.

"We have washing machines in Nepal too," said Ramesh looking at me like I was freak for telling them something they were perfectly aware of.

I thought I was educating them in western practices, and I failed. What I actually managed to do was rub their nose in the fact life at the orphanage was poor. The boys went to school with richer children so of course they knew. They probably had their noses rubbed in this fact on a daily basis.
I suppose a washer was too expensive to have at home and not a good investment as there were so many other things could be bought, like food, clothing, and essential items.
The boys helped me hang up my smelly washing and I sheepishly tried to retract my stupid statement.
I found it a bit weird young boys hanging up my smalls in the sunshine. None of them seemed bothered except Anil.

"What are these?" he said, laughing at my red knickers edged with lace. *"Do you wear these?"*

"Yes," I repliedm and he walked off shaking his head pointing at my pants and sniggering with Habir.

I needed something to make me feel feminine amongst the gaggle of snotty boys. I'd bought the red ones many months before my attempt to snare Liam, other than that I don't think I'd worn them.
After the knicker washing fun, the four younger boys and I walked into the river again. The big ones stayed at the home and had my phone to watch a movie.

181

As we walked the boys said they'd had no volunteers for six months as everyone goes to the girls' orphanage. Probably because it's only an hour from Kathmandu, not seven to nine hours like Pokhara. I also think it's because most volunteers were young girls in their twenties who don't want to be with the boys as they need lots of energy put into them. I was loving it though.

The boys liked having volunteers because having a volunteer equalled getting spoilt!

I was financially secure, although less than I had been, so a few treats here and there wouldn't hurt the boys. Plus, if I spoiled them, they would show me the best tourist sites. I met two female British dentists who didn't share my enthusiasm for giving the boys sweet treats.

"You shouldn't give them sugar," said one.

"No, there aren't many proper dentists and the ones that they do have in Nepal are expensive, you're just creating a bigger problem!" said the other.

"That's why we are here, to help educate families of good teeth brushing and stop them losing teeth," said the first dentist.

They were lovely women, but I felt well and truly told off. I hadn't realised that my generosity would cause problems. They were right though, looking around at the many toothless smiles, oral hygiene didn't appear to be a top priority.

We took the bus into town, which was full of trekking tourists, and hired a boat to venture around the stunning lake and visit the temple on an island. Lakeside was beautiful. The Annapurna mountain range enveloped the lake, letting off a radiant blue hue, and gleaming against the orange sun it was particularly striking at dusk.

I want to say the boat adventure was pleasurable and I'm sure if I'd taken it alone and rowed gently around the lake it would have been. However, with a group of boisterous boys, it was more like survival. My time was spent preventing the boat from capsizing, stopping them from pushing each other in the water, preventing them from standing up and plunging into the ice-cold lake beneath us. I was also ensuring we were going in the right direction and wasn't sure I knew where that was.

"Sit down Ridesh! Stop fighting Habir and Samil!" the brothers were always fighting. Most of my time was spent at the orphanage stopping Habir, the older sibling, from bashing the Samil, his younger brother.

"SIT DOWN!" I yelped, as the boat slowly tipped to the side letting in water and soaking my feet and legs. My leggings were wet, my bum was wet, and I was soaked. I couldn't help but laugh at the little scamps. Naughty as they were, they were just having fun, and who was I to kill their fun?
We rowed across to a temple on an island in the middle of the lake. It wasn't quite an island but a mound of land, cultivated with a strategically placed Hindu temple set there to trap tourists.
On arrival, we were accosted by people selling things. Nodding Buddhas, postcards, Hindu statues, orange flower garlands, can of drinks, you name it they had it on that little hill.

I went in and was disappointed to find discover it was just a shrine, nothing particularly remarkable. I donated some cash, did a little prayer, and received an orange dye Tika spot on my third eye in return. The boys were outside looking bored, they wanted to run around and play, not come here for the millionth time in their short lives.

"Mother, we are hungry, we want to go into town," said Ridesh.

183

The boys were surprisingly calmer as we rowed back. The prospect of a good meal made them better behaved.

After the boat trip, the cheeky monkeys asked to go to a really posh touristy restaurant.

Just to put it in perspective; they usually eat two meals of Daal Baat per day and share a jug of lukewarm water. If they were lucky, they may get double boiled rice.

Saturday, they have a bit of bony chicken, and Thursday half an egg. Their dining room resembles a scene from a Dickens novel with sparse long tables and benches, and a cold hard food soiled floor. I was waiting for one of the boys to demand,

"Please Mother, I want some more."

The theatrical me was conjuring up images from playing Widow Corny, the workhouse matron, in a recent production of Oliver. I loved the role but she's an absolute bitch, which I wasn't. I had a soft touch and the boys knew this.

I slipped into the restaurant with my wet boots and four dirty looking dishevelled boys. The waiter came around and smiled, like he'd seen these boys several times before in a similar state. Something told me I wasn't first volunteer to get soaked and tricked into taking them for food.

They ordered chips, chicken, a 7-inch pizza each, sprite, and coke. I had a green tea and peanut Sadako.

"Why you did not eat this pizza, Mother?" said Ridesh.

"Ridesh Sweetheart, we can have this food every day in England," I replied.

"Everyday. Wow, this is my dream," said little Samil, salivating at the prospect.

"This is why English people are fat," chuckled Anil.

184

Anil was right, they had so little money, yet their diet was far healthier than most of the kids I knew back home.

We walked back to the home, and I bought them a spinning top each. Simple pleasures, but no wonder they loved volunteers! When we arrived back all laughing and joking, Ramesh and Tika were both waiting by the door.

"You had a message while you were out," said Ramesh with a severe look on his face. He turned away and looked at the floor.
"Who's Mrs Logan?" he asked.

"My neighbour, my lovely neighbour," I quietly replied looking at the wall not wanting the boys to see my face.

I knew what was coming next. I didn't need to be told. Ramesh passed me my phone, and I read the message.

"Elise, it's Paul here. Sorry to bother you, but I wanted to let you know that Auntie passed away a few hours ago. It was peaceful, and she fell asleep, and we were with her. Thanks for all you have done for her over the years and sorry we only met you towards the end of her life. She always spoke about you and Steve with such affection, love Paul."

I sat looking at my phone for what seemed like forever. *'Mrs Logan's gone'* I thought. I knew she was on her way out, but I wanted to take some pictures and show her my boys. I wanted to share my Nepal trip with her as I'd done so many times before.

Who would take an interest now? There was no one left.

End of another era and yet another cue to get my arse in gear and get on with my life a sign to stop wallowing.

I spent the evening in my room on the hard, wooden bed, the mattress was so paper thin there's was no point in having it. The boys were playing a game in the stark grey walled T.V. room. It was hardly a T.V. room, being as the T.V. wasn't actually working.

Susila seemed to be unhappy with me taking the boys out for lunch as dinner had been a disaster. All except Ramesh and Tika had left their food. Leaving food was a sin in these parts where it was in such short supply. Susila had every right to be angry with me, especially given her family background. She'd also spent at least an hour cooking it and earlier we'd eaten like kings and hadn't invited her to come along.

Oops!

I felt part guilty and part rebel, I was sure Mrs Logan would approve, I thought, as I smiled inside thinking of that feisty old bird.

The boys had mentioned an army guy that volunteered for three months. They told me how he made things with them and proudly showed me the garden they'd created. They said that they liked him and missed him. That's what the boys needed, an excellent male role model and someone who they could aspire to be like.

Not me, I was just Mother who couldn't keep up at football and hill walking. I've got to admit, I was a bit jealous of army boy.

My thoughts turned to Liam – I could see him doing this stuff. He would love it, just getting stuck in. It was right up his street, and the boys would like him too. He was full of fun and very active. Not sure he was any good at football though, in fact, I'm sure he was terrible, but he'd give it a good go just to get involved.

He was bouncy and childlike like a twelve-year-old boy, unreliable, and downright annoying. The boys would have loved him. I'd come away to forget about him, but everything reminded me of him. I barely knew the guy in comparison to Steve. Although based on revelations about Steve, I'd spent years with someone that I didn't know at all.

186

Liam would have sorted Samil's car out, no problem. Unlike me who fumbled to put a plaster on as it gushed with blood, I was useless with anything medical, I was useless at most things nowadays.

I'd thought about him a lot while playing with the boys.
Before Christmas I'd tried to avoid looking at Liam's Facebook profile after un-friending him. I couldn't stand to see what he was doing and didn't want to see pictures of him and the girlfriend. Was I a child? With a bit of spare time on my hands, I did what any young girl obsessed with her favourite pop star would do, I stalked him on his social media accounts.
His profile had said single in all the time I'd known him. But he'd been with her for 6 months. Wasn't he that bothered about her? I was hoping it had fizzled out or he'd been back up to his old tricks of being a player.
Maybe he was having second thoughts? I hoped he was having second thoughts. He didn't gush about her and apart from saying she was pretty he never said anything else nice. He couldn't lie about that, she was pretty, I'd seen pictures of her. He gave her no other compliments, but that didn't mean a thing. He never poured about anyone or anything. He struggled with emotions and it drove me mad. He'd already told me he didn't have romantic feelings for me and that I was just his mate.
I thought while he was still displaying single signs to the outside world, there was hope. Why was I so needy? I didn't need him or Steve to affirm I was a catch and the type of woman men would want. Why was I still seeking everyone's approval?
The trouble was, the more disastrous dates I went on, the more I needed Liam's approval.
I thought I'd go on social media and see what he was up to, what was he doing? Were there any small signs he might be interested in my travel.

NO!

Relationship status; in a relationship with her!

My heart sank, and I sobbed. I don't know why, because I knew she existed they'd been together a while. But this was like confirmation to the world. Mr Reserved *'I'm not getting attached'*, had a love life, and was now confident in announcing it to the world.
He wouldn't do that unless he was sure. He's a bit gung-ho with other things but not his emotions. I wondered if he'd told people about me, some stupid old bird he'd met online who wouldn't leave him alone. Bet he didn't. Bet he was too embarrassed.
I was a washed-up freaking embarrassment to him and myself, to everyone.
It was weird I wanted him, but I didn't want to be with him. Most of the time I wasn't entirely sure what I wanted him for, then at others I wanted to do things with him, riding bikes, watching a film, cooking together. Maybe I was just looking to cure my loneliness. I was sad.
So sad that I spent most of the trip throwing myself into things with the boys. Which was the purpose of the trip in the first place. I was determined to enjoy every minute with them and forget about that dickhead, the spider phobic wimp, I hated him.

Chapter 28
Swimming in the River and No Mirror Needed

I got up and swept and mopped the floors outside. The mop bucket of water was cold and grey with dirt and the tiniest drop of detergent that wasn't going to get much clean. This regular task of transferring filth and debris from one part of the floor to another seemed pointless to me. I had to remind myself where I was and the limited resources and sanitation that were available.

I prepared breakfast with Susila. The days veg-fry to accompany our Daal- Baat was cauliflower – the Nepali people found multiple uses for the cauliflower. I used every inch of the vegetable including the green stalk. The boys assured me was tasty once mixed with Garam Masala and chilli. It was. The green stalked chopped finely into small pieces and gently tossed in vegetable oil and spices was delicious.

It made me realise just how much we waste back home and just how lazy we were when it came to food preparations. Back in the U.K. I would opt for Tesco pre-bagged and pre-washed vegetables, cutting out unnecessary preparations.

This environment destroying practice favoured by all busy working families in U.K. made me realise my own behaviour.

This trip was making me question a lot of things:

- Excess food consumption
- The environment ruining practices
- Working too much
- Excess spending

All totally unnecessary and tiresome.

I hadn't seen a mirror since the hotel in Delhi, which by orphanage standards had been opulent. Quite frankly, at this point in the trip, I didn't care. I wasn't wearing makeup and wasn't bothered. I love my make-up and getting dressed up, but there was no point there. I was enjoying the freedom and lack of judgement.

I was stripped back and loving every second.

There was absolutely no need for mirrors at the orphanage and just like the wicked queen in Snow White, I received a daily update from the boys on how I looked.
I don't even need to chant, *'Mirror, mirror on the wall, who is the fairest of them all'*. From the boy's reaction I knew it generally wasn't going to be me.
Two days before, the boys told me I looked tired, stressed, and my hair was too short. Women in Nepal appeared to have long hair. I had ugly feet, although that wasn't really a surprise, one of Sophia's names for me was hog toes.
To them, I was an old lady. I knew what Mrs Logan was talking about when she said she didn't like looking in the mirror. However, this one particular morning I felt alive and vibrant, I felt happy for the first time in a long time. I walked out into the crisp morning air.

"Good Morning, Mother. How are you today?" said Ramesh in his usual charming tone.
"Mother you look different, your face looks pretty today."

I wasn't sure whether to be flattered or offended. Nepali bluntness was endearing and being from Yorkshire I admired a direct approach. The boys didn't realise that by western standards that their usual comments would be deemed offensive, it was just their way. Lies were not learnt and that also stretched to saying exactly what they thought. The truth was, I had started to settle into my environment. I knew on most days I looked terrible and wouldn't have usually put the bins out in such a state at home let alone the school run. So, there was absolutely no need for a mirror. We took loads of selfies, especially with Ramesh the selfie model, just so I knew just how bad I looked.

Once again, I took the small boys swimming in the river. They swam and caught fish and played for about 3 hours. Those poor de-oxygenated fish they kept bringing me in various water filled sprite bottles, in order to salvage them, I made them put them back in the water.

On the way to the river, I bought the boys snacks; two boys had dried noodles using the powder flavouring like a condiment to flavour the dehydrated snack. Apparently, these were their favourite snack of choice. I thought it looked like prison food.

Two of the boys had sweets, a treat I'm sure Sophia would have preferred.

The boys didn't get many treats, but they always shared. Regardless of how hungry they were, they handed out their treats for others.

They always shared with each other, without being prompted and every 5 seconds were saying, '*you want, you want?*' to me.

Without much in the world, these boys were selfless and considerate. They didn't need teaching how to share, they just did. It was an inherent part of the culture. Not once did I hear those boys say '*Mine*' or '*Get your own*'. Phrases that are all too common in the affluent western world.

Although I've been brought up and lived most of my life in the U.K. I have an aversion for the British custom of being a selfish eater. People who sit and only eat their meal and never allow someone to take from their plate, the type of people who order a takeaway and only eat their own. I don't understand it, food is meant to be shared and is a social thing. The boys knew all about sharing and appreciated the food they were offered.

Over the past few days I'd started to speak to them individually and get to know them properly. They shared their family stories. They were all from different villages across Nepal. Some had no parents, some have just one parent, in some instances, the Father, who has to work. Some had both parents still alive living in extreme poverty. Families with too many mouths to feed couldn't afford to look after their children and were left with limited options, so either forced them

191

into prostitution, child labour, or out on the streets to fend for themselves.

One thing for sure was they loved the Happy Home and were grateful for their opportunity to live there.

I was proud of Asim and his family and what he had done to give these boys a chance.

At the river, the boys were playing happily skimming stones, while I sat on the bank sunbathing and reading my book. I was a slight distance away from them, but they were within sight.
When along came two men and took the two smallest boys, Samil and Ridesh, off for a walk towards a woodland area. I shouted after them,

"Boys! Boys where are going?" but was ignored mainly because I can't speak Nepali.

Call me overprotective, and maybe because I'm from a paedophile obsessed UK culture where news bulletins are set to scare any parent with an under 16-year-old, but I have a mistrust of strange men talking to children. My very British obsession with every strange man being a predatory child abductor kicked in.
During my entire childhood I was told never to speak to strangers, especially men. I grew up in the aftermath of the Yorkshire Ripper, Myra Hindley, and Ian Brady and the Wests.

"Oi. Oi!" I ran across the river.
"Where are you going? You're taking my boys!" I shouted. I fell in the river, soaking my trousers and cutting my arm. I was panicking, I was responsible for these boys and what if they fell into the hands of a serial killer or paedophile.
"Come back here. I'm your Mother! Listen to me!" I yelled.

The boys looked at me awestruck like I was some deranged woman and carried on walking towards the woodland. I looked deranged with my bleeding arm, wet trousers, and my hair all over the place. I didn't look like I could look after a few small boys.

"We get cigarettes for them," said Ridesh.

"No! You don't! You don't get cigarettes!" I panicked.
"They get their own cigarettes! They are grown men; they can go and get their own!" I screamed, partly scared, partly angry. They carried on walking.

The men took the boys into the woodland and it was about two minutes before I caught up with them. The men handed over money to the boys, and the boys ran off to the shop. I stopped there scowling and shouting at the men,

"What did you do? What did you fucking do to my boys?"

They were about forty or fifty years old, weathered looking and dirty, obviously land workers, it was hard to put an age on Nepali country people. They looked at me and laughed. I felt like a stupid deranged old hag who had lost the plot. In truth, the men hadn't had enough time to do anything untoward. Whatever seedy plan they had was thwarted by my crazy protective momma act.
The other boys told me it was standard practice asking kids to go and run errands, getting a beer or cigarettes in return for chocolate and money. Something I put a stop to while I was there.
The boys probably disliked me for it but at the very least it was taking the piss, and at the most to could have been far more suspicious. These boys were orphans and were vulnerable. Who knows what happened in the past or what will happen in the future should a protective adult not be present?

When we got back, Susila had her new lipstick on and was wearing a necklace, she'd also brushed her hair. I heard the rice man was doing his weekly delivery, so I'd joked she had made an effort for him. She laughed hysterically and hugged me tight, holding her bony body against mine in a friendly embrace.

Then she said she'd never marry again; having only had one husband and being 27 I found this sad. She was so in love with her husband and couldn't imagine being with anyone else. Her options would have been limited to other potential widows who were usually a lot older than her, maybe by as much as 40 years.

Some of the poor families in Nepal have a traditional view towards marriage as a Hindu.

As I was at the boy's orphanage, I only had exposure to two women, Susila and Nani. Both had made me think about women in particular from rural Nepal and their treatment. Actually, in both instances, the women are treated well and not excessively over worked. Asim has a good heart and looks after them, but the story would have been different in different hands.

Lives of Nepali women don't mirror those of the emerging world, and practices were set to keep women firmly in their place as they had done centuries before. A female child is seen as a financial burden on a family as they have to be fed and watered and paid for, only to not contribute then eventually leave the household to live with their husband's family.

For this reason, many young girls are sent to the cities to work as domestic servants for the richer middle-class Nepali people. They spend their days cooking and cleaning, and the school age girls go to school and get an education. I'm not sure how productive they could be at school after hours of domestic work.

Another reason that uneducated women end up alone is due to the Hindu belief that widows are cursed. They are seen as witches. Because a women's role is tied to the care of her husband, if the husband dies before her, and heaven forbid he dies young, the widow is treated with abject cruelty. This was the case with Susila. Often, she is beaten in public by her in-laws and during the funeral rites is abused and forced to remove her jewellery and all signs that she was a married woman. She can never again wear the colour red, the colour of married women, as a way to shame her. Again, these are very complicated and ancient traditional believe systems and I am not disapproving of Hindu religion or the people that follow it, but the oppression of a living being is never acceptable. Tradition or not.

All systems managed by humans have flaws and there are some gaping flaws in this society.

Asim's and his family discovered Susila living in extreme poverty in a remote Himalayan village. After losing both parents, many siblings and finally her husband, she was left to live with her late husband's parents. There she was treated like a modern-day slave, her body emancipated by starvation and extreme vigorous working conditions. She couldn't produce milk for her baby son. They were both seen as a burden on the family, not because the family were horrible people just because they were poor and it was a matter of survival.
Susila told me she wanted to learn better English, so I agreed to have a few hours together every day learning English while the boys were at school. She needed as much love as much as the boys did, probably more as she didn't have anyone.

My life was starting to look comfortable in comparison. Mine was all temporary, and all the heart ache, the manipulation, the unrequited love, was nothing.

At least I had a family who loved me and supported me.

There are many people doing amazing projects and helping people across Nepal. One person who cares passionately about the lives of poor Nepali women is Katherine Demsky, an American woman. I met Katherine on Facebook through a female travellers network. Katherine is working on various women's projects across the country.

She has asked what the women at her projects want from life and here were the responses:

• I want to help my children with their homework.
• My kids are living abroad and if I want to visit them, I need to be able to read and count.
• I am too afraid right now to fly abroad to visit my children so I am learning to read English so that I can make the journey.
• My kids work with me in the household and cannot go to school every day, so I want to help them learn when they miss classes.
• I need to learn how to use a phone and buy mobile data to call my children who are still in the villages. I need to learn to text because it is less expensive than making a call.
• I know when I turn 17 my employer will fire me and tell me to leave their house because this age of girl is too difficult to control. So, I need an education for when I lose my job and home. Or else I will have to go back to the village and my parents will make me get married so that I am not a burden in their home.
• I am a member of my neighbourhood women's group and want to run for office. But officers need to be able to read and give speeches, so I am learning to read and write in Nepali to help my community.
• I also am a member of the women's group and want to take a micro-loan from the group, but they told me I have to learn some math before they will give me a loan.

Katherine said she loves hearing these women talk about the future and runs classes in Kathmandu for women to learn English and express their feelings in a non-judgemental environment.
I'd love to take it a step further and work with volunteers taking the classes to the rural villages. This is a trickier project to manage as families and traditions get in the way of progress.
Women were vulnerable but so were young men, men who could fall into the wrong hands and end up in crime or on the streets. They also needed educating in how the modern world was working. Without modernising men's attitudes towards women, the future won't change.

196

After dinner, Tikka, the oldest boy and I went up to lakeside town, and I booked an exciting trip.

We talked about his long-term career aspirations; I wrongly assumed he wouldn't have any. I asked what will happen when he leaves home and has to fend for himself. I was a little bit worried about him. He seemed such a sensible young man and would be an asset to any company and I didn't want him getting lost in the world undoing his education and all of Asim and the home's hard work.

He said he may have to live with his family in the countryside, and went on to describe the walk he took from the bus in the town to get to her home near to the Chinese border. It sounded very remote and not somewhere a sixteen-year-old man could survive.

Tika was very modern, he had a mobile phone, he liked rap music, and he knew a lot about the modern world, mainly things he'd learnt from other volunteers.

I didn't think returning to live with his Grandmother and Uncles was a very good idea. His family were poor, and I suspected he would be used as a meal ticket to con and trick people. He was a good boy, but we can all be influenced by our environment. He had so much potential to do well.

I told him to stay in Pokhara as there will be more opportunity and he might meet someone from Europe who will offer him a job or sponsorship. I liked Tikka, he was a sensible boy.

He said he might like to try out for the Gurkhas as he met the qualification criteria because he originates from the Gurka region.

We went for dinner to Rosemary kitchen, a quaint wooden clad place specialising in western food. Eating dinner with just me and the elder boy seemed a very civilised thing to do, bearing in mind the boys would be eating Daal Baat in the cold back at the orphanage.

I wanted to take the opportunity to have a good chat with him, free from the younger boy's silliness. At the orphanage he always seemed out of place, not a boy but not quite a man. He assumed the role of a Father, but he didn't have a father figure or role model as such.

197

Tika ordered a pizza and sprite. I enjoyed his company and was starting to wonder what life would have been like I'd had children younger and had a Son.

I liked boys; they were on the whole emotionally uncomplicated. They didn't use bitchiness to argue. Boys had good fight and forgave each other.

'Why did they grow up to be such dickheads in adulthood?' I contemplated as I thought about Steve and Liam.

On that day I thought about why we did things to impress and please others and how this had somehow summed up my life. I was the conditioned child desperate to please her Mum, desperate to please a husband, and then when left without any of them I had no one left to please or impress. My whole life I'd spent showing off and getting attention and now I didn't know why. A whole life of buying things and being things that I didn't know how to be, the boys helped me discover myself.

Chapter 29
My Day Off and Acting Like a Tourist

Strictly speaking, there was no official day off at the Orphanage. Volunteers could come and go as they pleased, providing there was some volunteering taking place. Everything was very relaxed, and no one questioned too much.

I liked the boys and loved playing out with them, so I spent most of my time with them. After all, that's why I went there. When the boys were at school and the chores were done, there wasn't a lot to do. I couldn't really build anything and the bit of gardening I managed to do was pathetic.

So, I managed to find a day when the boys were actually at school, only the 4th in the time I'd been there. I kept questioning why all the other kids seemed to be at school, so much so the boys were sick of hearing the broken record.

I was just suspicious.

"Our school is better!" Ramesh exclaimed.

"I doubt that, you're never there," I replied

He smiled at me with his sweet charming smile, that kid was going to break some hearts, such a beautiful looking boy.

I imagine the graduation age would be about thirty, judging by the amount of days they have off.

Later in the week, I'd planned to spend more time helping Susila with her English more, so wouldn't have much time to do the tourist stuff.

When Tika and I went into town I booked to go on a helicopter ride to Annapurna base camp. It was a second-best option as I really wanted to do Everest base camp, just to say I'd been.

But at a £1,000 for 2 hours I thought it expensive and a bit steep considering the poverty in Nepal, and I was getting out of the habit of showing off. Nobody cared and taking a helicopter was hardly a challenge. I vowed one day I really wanted to see Everest that I would walk to base camp. That would be a challenge.

I'd also planned a treat for the boys and wanted to save my money for that. I'd always planned to treat the boys despite the fact I was pretty broke. Ridiculous and frivolous, but my poor financial situation was temporary, and I could always find a way to make money when I got back home. I always broke my back to make money, something that was more difficult for the boys and poorer or uneducated people in rural Nepal.

I was assured my trip to Annapurna was still going to be awesome. Annapurna is the tenth highest mountain in the world. Nepal has eight of the top ten – Nepal is bloody hilly. These were not Ben Nevis or Snowdon territory; these were something else.

I walked for 90 minutes into town and took a taxi up to the airport ready to take my helicopter ride. I didn't know what to expect and I packed my backpack for every weather eventuality. Sun cream, waterproofs, extra socks, extra sweater, woolly hat.

I got to ride in front of the helicopter, and I don't like helicopters. I remembered Steve and I took one over Manhattan a few years before. I hated every second, it was the worst most nail-biting experience of my life. I kept thinking about the twin towers and how if there was an engine failure we could come crashing down onto a skyscraper below.

This time with only the thought of crashing into a mountain, which seemed a more palatable option than the New York skyscraper one, I quite enjoyed it. I joked I was the co-pilot, talking into my imaginary radio, much to the amusement of the lovely German family and woman who shared the flight.

The helicopter flew over some beautiful mountains giving off a blue hue, and finally I was close to the mountains I'd been looking at in the distance every morning.

We landed and the rotary blades were still running, I ducked under them and headed over to a wooden building on the top of a slight hill, which looked like a cafe and hostel. I sat down upon the hill drinking mint tea in the sun, awestruck by the scene. I took photos, but they will never be able to capture just how amazingly stunning the place was. The memory etched on my brain for an eternity. I never want to forget the beauty of being up close to the Annapurna range.

I didn't need a pair of Louboutin shoes, dick pics, or sex in a posh hotel room when I had this amazing sight to look at. This was far more exciting.

It's a weird environment, being stuck half way up one of the tallest mountains in the world. It's boiling hot and freezing cold all at the same time. I was getting a tan and freezing my bits off all in one sitting. I don't ski, and my one disappointing attempt in Lapland told me I should never try it again, but I imagine all skiers experience this. I moved further around to get a better view of the enormous Annapurna mountain top. I sat on the snowy floor and could feel my bum getting wet. It was an awesome sight, and I thought how I wouldn't have been here if I hadn't wanted to escape. I made the odd decision to come because home life was just too painful.

For the first time I thanked Steve for leaving and Liam for being a non-committal prick. If things had turned out differently, I wouldn't have ever been here, in the mountains seeking adventure and new experiences.

My mind took me back to an incident that had happened when we moved to our new home. We lived around the corner from the family home.

Sophia, ran into the kitchen;

"Mummy, Daddy said he's coming and sounds so angry," she said nursing her phone which was vibrating from ringing and ringing.

Steve wasn't really supposed to come around to our home due to an aggressive incident that had happened a few months before.

"He won't come here Sweetie, don't worry," I said trying to reassure my daughter.

I actually believed it; he wasn't going to come to the house.

30 minutes later there was a loud knock at the door. My daughter ran to the window.

"It's Dad, it's Daddy!"

"Let me in Sweetie, let me in, I need to know you are safe. I don't think you're safe," he said in a slightly sinister tone.

"Don't let him in Darling," I said urging my 9-year-old to come away from the door.

"Let me in you little liar, you lied to me," his tone changed to aggression.
"You all lied to me, you all fucking lied!" he hit on the door while screaming at us.

He continued to kick and punch the door.

All the time my daughter kept saying I'll go home with Daddy and he'll stop. This is because I lied to him. We didn't tell him where we were living.

We didn't need to; she still saw him, and circumstances had changed.

It wasn't because she lied. This wasn't about my Daughter or how much he cared. This was about losing control of me. This was about me having strength in numbers, I'd move in with my friend, who had more neighbours. More people to suss him out, more people who could see him for what he really was; a massive narcissistic bully. He wasn't angry I'd moved and not told him. He was angry I'd moved, and he was losing less and control over me. He was angry that his manipulating tactics didn't wash anymore.
Then he tried to reason with us, opening the letterbox and shouting,

"Sweetie, I love you, please come home with Daddy."

"I need to go with him Mummy or he'll get more angry. Mummy he's so angry with me," she sobbed uncontrollably, attempting to find the keys for the downstairs door. The door he was trying to kick in.

His girlfriend sat in the car, in shock and shaking her head. Probably realising for the first time she'd been sold a dream but was living a nightmare. She was clearly under his control. No woman would drive her partner to house and watch him attempt to frighten a little girl and threaten to kill her mother.
For the first time, I felt sorry for this woman. A woman who didn't know how to manage him, a woman who looked frightened and under his control.

I'd dialled 999 and the police arrived and put him in the car for a chat.

They came in to interview me and then my daughter.

They must have released him at some point because he started to call Sophia on her phone.

Harassing her, trying to speak to her.

The policewoman answered;

"What do you want?"

"I just want to say goodnight to my Daughter," he said, sounding and looking rather pathetic and drunk.

It's funny how excessive alcohol has the ability to render people into pathetic states. This aggressive man, the man who had threatened to

203

kill us an hour before, was nothing but a pathetic boy who'd lost control and was now begging a police officer for contact with his child. A child who'd also seen him in a different light.
All respect and dignity had gone.

"Sir, your daughter is going to bed, you can speak another time."

Narcissists are scary creatures, but I wasn't scared. What I saw in front of my eyes was a weak-willed man, attempting to clutch on and control someone he didn't know anymore. A person who was getting braver and stronger.
He had no one that cared about him really. He hadn't built solid foundations that would last long term. His family didn't care. Yes, they may have participated in the drama but only because it was short term entertainment, his girlfriend was under his control, and once she had freed herself would feel the same as me.
He was going to be a lonely old man. I saw before me a wreck of a man, a man who was once beautiful and charming, a man who had charisma and money, a man I'd once loved and spent a long time with.

He wasn't any of those things anymore, he was a fraud.

I wasn't scared at all of his actions, in fact, little did he know but he was actually making me stronger. On the outside I looked weak and vulnerable. On the inside I was a tower of steel and determination.
.
My spirituality gave me reason to believe I was experiencing this because good things were to come.

And just like the end of the Emperor's New Clothes, people were started to see the naked truth. I'd exposed him. Or should I say, he exposed himself.
My tactic for dealing with a narcissist is to let him think he'd won. Don't argue or fight about small things, allow them to have small

204

victories but create boundaries, boundaries you are not prepared to step out of. Be consistent, because inconsistency is fuel for them to pick holes in. Avoid getting over emotional and look towards the long term with short term coping strategies.

My tactic was to play dead. I ignored him, or I would only answer questions that were important to Sophia. Make him think he's got you and you are ruined because he'll go away. Like dealing with a predator, once the chase is over and they've nibbled the best bits, you are no use to them.

Make plans in the background, exit plans. Use a few trusted people to help you.

Don't write anything down that they can access.

Never ever confront them. Narcissists rarely get hit or into trouble. Teflon Kings and queens.

Meditate, practice self-hypnosis, take a long bath, have a peaceful walk.

If you can get out or away, join a club or take a small trip.

My favourite was a horse box stay in St Ives, very cheap and peaceful setting.

If you can't get away, escape in a book. Or better still, write or draw your own. Use your imagination to take you into a pleasant land, a different land that is free of drama.

When conflict occurs imagine you hovering over the situation and looking at it as an outsider. Imagine it's a play or a soap opera.

I didn't hate men and I didn't subscribe to the *'all men are the same'* mantra. Men aren't all the same, just as women aren't.

I'd just made bad choices.

I knew in my heart of hearts there was a lovely man out there for me. A man who didn't lie or cheat and who would love me and my daughter. I wasn't looking for him and would be happy to wait a while.

After about forty-five minutes up there, we were called back to the helicopter. Except the woman on her own couldn't be found anywhere. There was a small search party looking for her, she couldn't have gone far. I think helicopter pilot was a bit worried she's fallen off the cliff face while taking a selfie.

Twenty minutes later, the woman was being dragged, I mean literally dragged by her arm, and thrown onto the aircraft by a Sherpa.

She had the most inappropriate outfit on for the excursion. I found the hilarity in this as she was wearing jeans, a thin long-sleeved top, a beautiful pashmina draped across her shoulders, flip flops, a full face of make up on, and was clutching a large designer handbag.

She looked freezing and embarrassed and the Sherpas were not impressed – less so was the helicopter pilot but all were too polite to say anything.

I gave her my spare sweater and some socks to put on.

Annapurna mountain is not a place you wear your best going out clothes. It's full of trekkers and old hippies, so no one gives a shit if you've got Prada, North Face, or Hemp on. They care if you're to dressed appropriately and risking your life by potentially getting hyperthermia.

Back at Lakeside I sat in the Glacier hotel cafe bar, one of the smartest places in Pokhara, and had a coffee and poached eggs as I'd missed my morning Dal Baat and dinner wouldn't be for another ten hours.

Three coffees later, I left and walked up to the Buddhist monastery, which was peaceful. A walk that took me well over an hour and was in

206

the opposite direction to the orphanage. I'd have to get a taxi back – there was no way I was walking back.

I arrived at the gates. There were people peddling their wares, bracelets, necklaces, spices, nodding Buddhas: anything and everything.

"It's ok lady, we take Indian rupees," said one vendor.

'I should imagine they take gold teeth and wedding bands if they are worth anything', I thought to myself.

There appeared to be a lot of stray dogs hanging around. Amongst all the self-disclosure I've revealed in this book, what I forgot to mention is my fear of big dogs.

This place was like my worst nightmare, snarling rabid dogs everywhere. My heart was in my mouth and even if I wanted to buy anything, I couldn't for fear of being attacked. Another fear confronted on this trip and another step nearer to getting well.

Through the gates it was empty and peaceful, except I could hear a faint chattering of the novice monks who were on the balcony of their quarters. I assumed that monks never spoke and had to take a vow of silence. However, these kids were bloody noisy they were only about ten or eleven years old and in my experience kids of that age can't be quiet for too long regardless of any vow. The boys at the orphanage would have made terrible monks, they were far too boisterous, cheeky, and loud.

I wondered why such small children were placed into such an unusual environment. I mean, I'm not sure it was a lifestyle choice for them. It couldn't be, no child would choose the life voluntarily.

I think the monasteries, just like the orphanage, were there to create solace and a safe place to live for these children. I think many of them were also orphaned or street children. I missed the meditation by about ten minutes, so decided I'd return in a few days' time to meditate. I was getting in the habit of meditation and my spirituality was getting more attuned.

I wandered around the walled gardens of the monastery and came across a little old lady just sat outside. We communicated through the language of smiles and nods.

She took me up to the pray wheel and took my hand and placed it on the wheel. She spun it dragging my hand across all the barrels. She chanted, *'Om, namah, shivah'* and repeated this several times, urging me to copy her. After the initial embarrassment, looking around to see who was watching, and then realising she was serious about this I started to chant, *'Om, namah, shiva'* whilst rolling my hand across the carved cylinders of the small pray wheel.

Then she held my hand and ushered me inside the monastery where she introduced me to a giant pray wheel. The wheel went from the top of the ceiling to the bottom of the floor and was around 2 metres wide. We both spun the wheel chanting *'Om, namah, shivah'*. It was an initially awkward, but latterly a relaxing experience. The chant allowed me to clear the noise in my head and breathe deeply. This Buddhist life was definitely something I could get used to.

I ended the day in the rosemary cafe with Mo-Mo and green tea and did some shopping for Sophia. Not sure what was going to await me when I got back.

Chapter 30
Surprise for the Boys!

I spent time before breakfast doing homework with the boys. To be honest, being asked at 6am to write four pages in English on why computer programming language is essential to the modern world really hurt my head. All lessons in school were taught in English, no subjects were taught in Nepali language, other than Nepali. I was surprised at the proficiency of the boys English and they would rival any European education.

The schoolwork was so difficult, and I think some of our kids in the U.K. would struggle, let alone in the second language. English is an essential part of education and knowing the language gives the boys greater social mobility, an opportunity to get a good job, and is the primary route out of poverty. Having a good grasp of English meant the boys could work away in other countries like Dubai and earn good money to send back to their families. Knowledge of English propelled them into a high class, the educated classes.

This is a luxury not given to many children in rural Nepal and for girls even less so. Boys are naturally given more privileges as they are seen are the bread winners in a family.

The boys told me about the different cultures in Nepal and why Nepali people have different faces. Bordered between India and China, there's a blend of cultures and the food reflects this too. There are a lot of Indian influences, particularly with lentil curries and the mix of spices but the Mo Mo is a popular dish which is more of a Chinese style dumpling. All food is spicy and staying at the orphanage, I didn't get to sample as much as I'd have liked.

The boys had this idea that all westerners are pale and obese and basically all look the same. They think we look ill and badly looked after. We were out in Lakeside and Ridesh spotted a very blonde pasty rotund woman who I suspected was German.

"Look they have the same face as you and they are fat too, just like you!"

209

How cheeky! I'd lost loads of weight at this point.

Feeling bruised by the small child's description of me, I got on my cultural soap box and I explained that in Europe we too have different cultures and that some English people can even look like them.

I showed them photos of some of my friends with Indian heritage.

"See Ridesh, we have faces similar to your face in England too," I said. "In fact, Ridesh is also a popular name amongst people of Indian heritage who live in the U.K."

He smiled and said;

"I didn't know that, I thought people in England were all fat and white."

Talking about this stuff in an innocent educating way is nice. We weren't being disrespectful or racist, just pointing out similarities and differences. I enjoyed our chats. The thing about kids is they aren't born to discriminate so they just point out what they see. This is truer of the Nepali orphans as they had no social conditioning so their responses were even more innocent.

After breakfast, I walked up to school with the boys and then walked part of the way to town. We took the bus for part, mainly because my feet were sore.

I went to the harbour bar in the Glacier Hotel. I liked it in there, although it's very touristy, it was part of the nicest hotel in Pokhara. I liked it more as it was such a contrast to the orphanage and sitting by the lakeside I could write.

Apart from the odd piece of childhood poetry, I'd never written. I never knew I could.

Going through hell and meeting Liam somehow inspired me. I had emotional outbursts of energy that were usually sparked by Liam turning up or even better ignoring me. Did it matter that he had a girlfriend and I was a little too obsessed with him? He was good for my writing, but I never told him.

I sat typing on my phone looking over the vast Pwewa lake and thinking. I imagined where I was in the world. I could picture a map, and I was situated right on the western side of the land locked country.

I ordered poached eggs and coffee and waited for Pradip to turn up who was going to help me surprise the boys. Since I arrived, the boys haven't had anything to do in the evening, so would take my phone and watch a movie on YouTube. With the nights being baltic, cold and dark, there was nothing for them to do, they'd go to bed just waiting for the next day.

It sounded like my life back home; a life filled with going to bed waiting for a new day.

They had an old T.V. which had been broken about six months. Looking at it, I wasn't sure it was salvageable. Apparently during the summer, which also turn out to be rainy season, they had taken it outside to watch because they were warm, however a rainstorm arrived and it blew up. I enjoyed Samil's very animated account of the incident as he propelled himself off the chair to indicate an explosion.

Hopefully with that lesson learned, I decided I was going to buy them a new T.V. I didn't have much money but compared to these boys I was a Queen.

Prad arrived and we took a taxi across town, not far from the big monastery that I'd visited the day before. Pokhara was a large sprawling city and I hadn't appreciated just how gigantic it was, until that point.

"Where are we going?" I said nervously, sat in a taxi with a strange man.

I was unsure of Prad and not knowing whether or not he was a bad guy. He didn't look like a bad guy, but I didn't know him very well, he could have been anyone. However, I did what I always do on meeting new men; I sized up whether I'd be able to knock him out should things become a bit out of hand. He was only small and quite podgy and with my basic boxing training and a decent upper cut, I decided I could probably floor him and therefore was probably safe.

I hadn't had this fear until I had a date in the U.K. with a rather lascivious Iranian boy who was 6ft 6in tall, it was that encounter that encouraged me to take up the boxing.

"We are just going here," he said politely. I think he was actually more wary of me and my exuberant brash personality, which was getting more and more confident every day.

We hung around looking at T.V.s, lots and lots of T.V.s. I just wanted one that worked and that the boys could watch. I wasn't bothered about anything else, in fact buying T.V.s bored me.

But no, both Prad and the T.V. shop man had me looking at the picture, listening to the sound, the shape of the T.V. I just wanted a bloody T.V. and wasn't really bothered what it looked like, as long as it bloody worked! I was getting so frustrated and I was buying it, not bloody Prad.

Knowing how some shops could rip you off over a here a basic working T.V. was fine. I didn't need to be wowed with science only to discover when I got it back, it didn't work. Whatever we bought was better than the 4 walls they had to look at.

We were in there for what seemed like hours and I started to sulk like a child. I just wanted to pay the money and get the hell out of there.

Finally, Prad negotiated a decent price for me. I could hear him bargaining and bartering. This was only a small T.V. but a luxury item for them. I'm hoping they look after it, as I'd planned to go back to check up the following year.

Prad and I arrived at the orphanage like Santa and his helper. I gathered all the boys in the main room, which was like herding cats.

"Mother! What is in the box?!" said Ramesh.

212

"Keep your nose out," I said tapping my nose.

Samil spotted the picture on the box.

"It's a T.V!" he screamed excitedly.

And as Samil said that, all the boys bounded towards Prad and the box. Prad put the box on the floor and the boys were trying to open it up.

"Let Prad set it up boys, and we can go and play table tennis," I said in an attempt to cause a distraction.

Out we went to play table tennis. In the twenty minutes, it took to get Prad to set it all up, the boys were constantly asking:

"Is that our T.V Mother?"

"Will you take it back to England?"

"When will it be ready to watch?"

"How much longer is Prad going to be?"

Eventually, Prad came out and said it was all set up, and the boys tossed aside the table tennis bats and ran inside. I thanked Prad and he invited me to his parents' home for dinner the next evening. I was thrilled to be invited.

Chapter 31
School Run

As usual, I got up and helped clean round. For those of you who know me well, I still hate cleaning and no trip for however long is going to change that. It's mundane, a waste of time, and there's so many more things to do. I think the same about watching T.V. I did the garden too which I also hate.

I'm not sure a lobotomy would change it let alone being thrown into a far-off land to look after a bunch of orphans. I did explain to one date that if he wasn't comfortable with mess and the odd bit of grime that we shouldn't pursue the relationship any further. If anyone is planning on marry me after reading this book, take note Darling – you need to be comfortable with mess!

Ramesh was constantly wearing my pink flip flops, so I offered him them when I leave. He seemed pleased about it. He'd already had my Nike trainers, as I wanted space in my rucksack to take a few trinkets back.

"But they're pink!" I said.

"I like pink," said Ramesh

"Do you have other pink things?" I said desperately trying not to impose my view of pink being a girl's colour.

"I like all colours and they're just shoes, Mother" he said looking confused.

Point taken, they were just shoes and judging by his other pairs were in a considerably better state.

Just shoes, I thought to myself, why can't I just see that?

214

I wanted to walk up to the temple at the top of the hill near us. It was about an hour and a half steep walk. I was all cocky and confident having blasted boot camp sessions prior to going out there. Once again, the boys did it in flip-flops and put me to shame. Suddenly the smugness around going boot camp had worn off. It was full of tourists up there.

My ass hurt, my thighs killed, and I needed a bath. This was high unlikely considering there was only an ice-cold shower available, the river, or a hose pipe, and I'd been a stranger to all of those since arriving.

The boys told me I had a kind heart, the T.V. had been a big factor, but I think they liked that I spoke to them as proper human beings and little Samil just wanted cuddles. The boys said they were going to miss me when I leave to go home. I wasn't convinced, knowing the boys I knew who I was, just another transient person passing by with a friendly smile for a few weeks. I would most definitely be forgotten by them after a few weeks.

We bumped into a group of small girls from the village who said,

"We think Samil loves you and wants a Mother."

He did, he was only a baby. He wanted someone to scoop him up and kiss his little cheeky chops, someone to love him and watch him dancing, to take an interest in his schoolwork. They all needed this to some extent and at that moment in time, I needed them just as much, if not more

I'm glad I didn't research Nepal before I went. I had my tour guides in the boys. It meant no plans or pre-judgement before I arrived – everything was a surprise. I remember previous trips I'd taken with Steve, trips that had been meticulously planned out, leaving little time to take in the environment and truly enjoy the experience.

Granted, I saw all the sights New York, San Francisco, Morocco, Rome, Paris you name it, I'd seen the sights. But only for a brief time before being whisked off the next one.

In Nepal, I was able to breathe, to take in the atmosphere, to gawp in awe at its wonder. Nepal had been a different experience entirely and I would do it all over again. It had been the best medicine for a troubled mind, a mind going through turmoil, my very own *'midlife illness tour'*. My one regret is not doing it sooner, there are a lot of things you learn about yourself when propelled into a foreign land with limited amenities and expected to toss your own worries aside to care for others.

I snapped out of my daydream and the boys and I walked down to Lakeside, we took the boat across the lake and had drinks and food for the final time. On the way back we bumped into the lovely Belgian family I met in a bar yesterday who wanted to buy the boys an ice cream each.

I was pensive and quiet, taking in my surroundings and for the final time, picturing where I was on a map of the world. After this, there would be no more boating trips with the boys, no more pizza and chips treat, no more coffee by the lake. I knew that the colours, the pictures, the sights, the noises and smells would be etched in my brain and felt deep in my soul for eternity.

I made the boys do the ninety-minute hike back to the Happy Home, it wasn't a particularly hilly walk, just long. We could have taken the bus, but I selfishly wanted to take in the sights of the dusty streets and watch the boys frolic and mess about a little longer.

We arrived back at the happy home sweaty and dishevelled and a very happy looking Sheru bounded in to greet us. I was in trouble with Susila because the boys didn't eat their dinner after their pizza and ice creams. It was the last time I'd get into trouble such antics.

I went to bed to write up my blog for the day while the boys sat watching *'Dance India Dance'* which can only be described as Bhangra's answer to Strictly Come Dancing.

I laid there thinking about my trip, the events that had happened back home:

- Mrs Logan was dead.
- Steve had a new home and new baby and therefore Sophia had a new sister.
- Liam was in a relationship.
- I was unemployed.

Where did any of this leave me? I could wallow, or I could take my experience and the events leading up to it and do something positive with my life.

Chapter 32
Food, Looking after Samil, and a New Pashmina

As per the usual routine I helped cook breakfast, soya and potatoes with Daal bat. I chopped tomatoes and crushed the garlic using a stone and heavy plate, like an ancient pestle and mortar. It's hard going, and I smashed my fingers a few times with the heavy stone. It smelled like a Saturday night at the local curry house. I liked the soya stuff as it was something different and more like meat, something I'd barely eaten since Christmas Eve. Although I put too much water in, and the texture was that of a squelchy wet sponge. I could feel it squelching and squeaking against my teeth as I took a bite to sample, but the flavour was good.

The boys and I went for a walk up in the hills singing Ed Sheehan songs, as we went.

Habir pushed over his little brother, poor Samil. Samil cut his leg badly and I spent the next twenty minutes trying to find something to clean the wound. I found some anti-bacterial gel in the bottom of my bag and a plaster and placed it over the cut, just as I'd done several days before when he cut his ear. Just the same as before no-one seemed to care. Boys were boys and they were expected to be and had to be tough.

After a couple of hours out with the boys, I went back to the home to teach Susila, who didn't seem too bothered about learning English. Gossiping with the local cow herding woman seemed to be hot on her agenda.

The cow herding woman was a rotund, portly figure of roughly around fifty years old, sporting a rather long navy-blue skirt and a red woolly cardigan. I was wearing a vest top and leggings; it was 25 degrees and boiling by U.K. standards. In that heat and with all those layers on, I should imagine the cow woman smelt as bad as the cows when she arrived home and eventually took her clothes off.

The boys gathered in the T.V. room and did their homework. I hovered round assisting them but spent most time with Habir. Habir needed the most support, but he was the most troublesome of the gang.

I'd been invited to spend the evening with Prad and his family. I thought it was a lovely gesture, so I took a bus up to Lakeside ready to meet him. Up in Lakeside I bought a new blue cashmere cardie, which was bargain at about nine pounds. I sat in a new bar in town, a very modern white and glass structure with perfect views of green field and the Annapurna range peaky out in the distance. The owner asked my opinion on what was missing. I suggested local live music. Quite frankly I didn't care, the bar was better suited to an Ibiza vista and looked out of place in Nepal.
It was geared up for tourists and not the real Nepali people I'd met, who didn't have the money to go out to such places. I did enjoy the chill out tunes and a small beer and watched the beautiful sunset while I waited for Prad and family to meet me. I think we'd agreed 8pm but I couldn't be sure. It was dark and I was already getting tired.
Prad eventually turned up and I was still wary of him, he seemed to have a leery look in his eye, although I had worked out, that in 'knock out ability' stakes he was perfectly safe. He turned up in taxi and we headed to his parents' home. It turns out that he had a Wife and Daughter in Kathmandont but rarely sees them due to working away. Prad's father was some sort of Nepali diplomat and they lived in a huge home in the centre of Pokhara. The home was clean and tidy with some modern furnishings. It was the first taste of luxury I'd encountered since leaving Asim's home in Kathmandu.
I took my shoes off as is the etiquette of entering all Nepali homes and was given a pair of slippers to wear. Prad's Father and Mother came to great me, followed by his two Sisters, who had been busy preparing food in the kitchen, and finally his English brother in law, Alan. Alan was from Manchester, a fellow northerner. I didn't feel so alien with him around and could speak in my normal voice without having to slow down any words or change my colloquial terms for more formal speech.

Prad had invited me to dinner to prove a point, that Nepali food wasn't all Daal Baat and squishy soya. I'd complained that the food at the orphanage was starting to get boring and I was craving something else. So, determined to prove a point and to show off his sisters' culinary skills, he invited me to dinner.

They cooked a Nepali style chicken curry, with chapattis and rice, and various other bits and pieces. I nibbled on salted almonds and drank whiskey with Alan while I waited for my dinner.

Prad wasn't wrong, the food was delicious, very spicy but very tasty. I continued knocking back the whiskey and talking to Alan and Prad about my time in Nepal. Obviously peppered with a few quips and comparisons about back home, something that only me and Alan understood. I really think sarcasm should come with English lessons. I left their home about midnight and took a taxi to the orphanage. Prad and Alan came with me as I was a lone female. I actually think that the taxi driver would have been more scared of me, than that pair. Alan was a slight man with a bad back and Prad was small and soft.

I was getting mentally stronger day by day, so help anyone who wanted to tackle me.

Chapter 33
Last School Run, Samil's New Bag, and the Guru

On my last full day in Pokhara with the boys I'd given them all a nickname. This was so I'd remember their characters. There were only six boys, in the end, Kiran went back to live with family for a few months until things settled down following the funeral.

I told the boys I was going to be sad as I was leaving. They said all the volunteers cry when they leave. I can understand why. I can't imagine how I'd feel if I'd stayed a few months, not a few weeks. I felt part of their family, like I belonged there.

We walked up to school and I attempted to fix Samil's broken school bag, but I only made it worse. The straps were hanging off and all his books toppled out onto the dusty road. The look on his little face was like his was disappointed in me and I'd already let him down once this trip by not watching his dace show.

Falling for this ever so subtle childish manipulation I felt guilty, I asked the boys to take me to a shop to get him a new one. Besides I'd fallen for greater manipulation than this, from two big boys in the U.K. who should know better.

We walked back to the shop on the corner by school and Samil pondered over the rack full of school bags before eventually choosing a Spider-Man one.

Having parent guilt for the second time in as many minutes, I ended up buying the boys a chocolate bar each. I liked the boys and wanted to spoil them rotten with things and love. I could feel my heart opening up the more time I spent with them. My heart had been so dead prior to the trip. It had been stamped on and rejected by two very different men.

These young men helped me see love again.

The boys tootled off to school, Samil showing off with his new bag.

I hopped on the bus and went to town as I'd planned on walking back. I didn't in the end. Most of the chores were done so I got the morning free to get some gifts and bits to take home. Plus, some new volunteers were supposed to be arriving.

I met up with Prad who took me to see a Guru guy to have a Reiki treatment. Alan had mentioned the previous evening that he had a bad back and that his energy system was out of kilter. He'd talked of a guy he visited on a regular basis to have Reiki treatments. I'd had Reiki back in the U.K. and I'm a huge fan. I'd not experienced it before Steve left and I didn't know what it was, but when faced with catastrophic stress I decided to give it a go.

There are sceptics out there, but I really believe we are energetic beings and that the treatment balances this out. It's always worked for me.

I knew I was going home and wanted to return home being the best version of myself.

The Guru guy lived in a large house behind the main street at Lakeside. I turned up on his doorstep and knocked on the large wooden carved door. Anticipation welled up in front of me and I was a bag of nerves, excited and sweating heavily.

A teenage girl answered the door in pyjama style clothing. She was a sweet smiling girl of about fifteen or sixteen.

"Take your shoes off and put them down here," she said politely. "My father will be with you shortly."

Oh, the Guru's daughter! I didn't expect him to have a daughter. Then my silly immature mind wandered, does that mean he's actually had sex with a woman?
Oh my god! I'm so inappropriate at times. I wanted to quieten my stupid noisy mental head.

With that image imprinted on my mind, in walked a man dressed from head to toe in an orange pyjama suit, looking like the Dalai Lama.

"You must be Elise?" he enquired.

Oh my god!! He sounded like the Dalai Lama! I almost pee'd my pants with excitement.

He took me upstairs to a roof top terrace and poured me a glass of water. He asked me to lay down on a wooden bed with the sun shining down across face and my torso. I was warm and comforted by its rays. The air smelled of incense sticks and I felt at peace.
He carefully draped a light blanket across my feet and asked me to close my eyes.
I closed my eyes and I drifted away. I could feel the tense energy lifted away from my body as he continued to work across various chakras.

I thought about how a few months earlier I had almost taken my own life.

Loneliness had set in and my mood was so low that I couldn't see a way out.

I was up then I was down. The ups were exhilarating, and the party loving me came out to play. The downs were macabre and gloomy, and the big black dog wafted over me. It had been going on too long and I was starting to think I had bi-polar disorder.
It had been a Sunday evening which seemed to be my normal lonely night. Sunday was a family night for everyone else, and I didn't have a family anymore. I didn't have a family nearby.

This one Sunday evening I had text everyone I knew and there was no response.

Liam had done another disappearing act and gone cold again. I put up with his behaviour because when he was around, he inspired me. He was also a good verbal punchbag. When I'd got fed up of bothering everyone else with my misery, there was always him to lash out at.

There was no point anymore. Everyone had their own lives, which seemed to be carrying on happily without me.

Sophia wanted to live with her dad because I was either in bed or out socialising, mainly drinking and picking up random men, not that she saw this behaviour.
Her Dad's house symbolised a family unit, a proper family with proper meals times and lots of children to play with. I could barely dress myself let alone create a family atmosphere and disciplined mealtimes.

Steve had threatened when I had the termination;

"Just you see, I'll set up a new family and Sophia won't want to be with you, you fat retard. You can't do anything thoroughly and properly, she'll see how useless you are," the words circled in my head.

These weren't only Steve's words but those of my Mother. I'd spent a childhood of being a failure because I wasn't perfect enough for her.Steve did exactly what he said he would, only the family had already been lined up long before I got pregnant. The family had already been in the pipeline before our split, he'd already planned his actions. Actions set to drive me insane. A terrible tactic he'd picked up in childhood from watching his Dad's cruelty to his Mum.
Depression took over me like a large dark cloud, weighing heavy on my mind, body, and spirit. I'd been stock piling paracetamol for a moment like this. I sat on my kitchen floor with them strewn all over. I took two tablets and a gulp of wine, then two more, and more wine.

224

I didn't like swallowing tablets so the thought of trying to take more was distressing me.

I wasn't considering family, Sophia or anyone who might have had a glimmer of love for me. All I could see was the horridness of the current moment and the future was a big, dark, empty hole of nothing.
I took the bottle of wine and downed the lot, necking it straight from the bottle. It was Chardonnay left over from a party I'd had. I hate Chardonnay, it's too tart and strong. I took two more paracetamol.

Then I felt sleepy, really exhausted. I staggered across the room landing flat on my head, so I was stretched across the white tiles of my kitchen floor.
I must have passed out because I woke feeling the cold floor against my skin. My head was heavy, like lead and I wanted to puke. I tried to get to the bathroom but instead projectile vomited across the kitchen floor. As I did, I yelped and cried, then I collapsed in a heap amongst the sick coated tiles.
I wallowed around on the floor for ages moving around so my body was covered in vomit, whilst crying my heart out.

Steve was right, I couldn't do anything right, I couldn't even successfully kill myself.

As the Guru finished his treatment, I could feel my mind clearing and the constant buzz I'd had in my body disappeared. I felt like I'd offloaded a ton of emotional weight. I slowly got up, drank my water and sat on the wooden bed.

"You are suffering from a lot of stress," said the Guru. "Your throat is very sore, like you want to say things and communicate but can't say what you really want, is that true?"

"Yes, that's very accurate," I said in a hushed tone.

225

"Your head is also very troubled, you have a lot in there that needs releasing," he continued.

"I know, but no one understands. I don't understand my life anymore," I said desperate for answers.

"You know something Elise? You had to go through this, this was your journey. You'll understand what I'm saying in time. Take it easy and meditate, your path is opening up and your strong enough to walk it," he finished his speech and walked downstairs ushering me to follow him.

'Thank you, goodbye.' I said, almost crying.

I paid him and spent the rest of the day thinking, in fact, I spent the last few days reflecting.

The next day I walked up to Harbour Bar for my coffee, and sat writing my 2018 goals, not resolutions. Resolutions never get achieved and have no finite date or actions set to them.
Many of my friends attempted to give up things: give up smoking, stop eating junk, stop drinking. All setting unrealistic and unattainable expectations.

Goals were things you were going to do, actions, tasks, activities with a tangible outcomes.

2017 had been a year of wasted time, energy and emotion. In 2018 I planned to do stuff, different things. One was to come back to Nepal with Sophia. The boys wanted to meet her, and she wanted to meet them too.

My list of goals:

- Study two things that take my interest.
- Get a new job, a more fulfilling one and one not for profit.
- Ditch the solicitor and represent myself in court.
- Take a writing holiday.
- Write blogs.

2018 was going to be a different year.

I grabbed a taxi back to the orphanage to teach Susila English for the afternoon. This had probably been the most rewarding thing I did and something I wish I'd spent more time on. The boys learnt English at school. She cleaned and waited around all day with only the occasional visitor from the rice man or the cow herding woman. I hoped for her own future that she would try to learn more with other volunteers, as it will give her a chance of getting out of poverty. Susila had never been to school and mainly spoke Hindi. Her Nepali wasn't brilliant either. She was very keen to learn and try her English out on the boys, even if they giggled when she didn't quite pronounce things right.
I went to bed early as it was too cold to sit up and watch a Bollywood film with the boys, but mainly because I didn't want to cry.
Relaxing in the sun having my 'Chakras' cleansed the day before was a lovely experience and The Guru did ask if I had a sore throat as he said my throat area seemed inflamed and stopped drinking too much coffee.
I got a sore throat from Samil and Habir who were constantly snotty, and my coffee habit was becoming worse than my alcohol drinking one. I wasn't an alcoholic, but I did have an unhealthy relationship with booze. By drinking coffee, I'd just replaced one bad habit for another. I promised myself I drink more green tea when I got back.

I was home sick and ready to see Sophia, I'd missed that pudgy face and cheeky smile. I'd missed her quick wit and kooky personality. She was my side kick, my mini me, and my reason for trying so hard to work through my troubles. She needed me, and I needed to be her

Mum once again. She was going to see a different Mummy returning, a strong Mummy, a role model. She was about to meet the Mum she hadn't met yet, the real me.

Christmas and the New Year passed me by, but I didn't care, it's my least favourite time of year anyway. There's too much pressure put on people to have a good time, to spend it with family, to spend money, eat too much and drink too much. At that point I'd had too much excess in my life.

It's was a wonderful experience and one I will always remember with great fondness as the trip that changed me and inspired me to write. I was hoping to return to Nepal later in the year with Sophia, finances permitting. Prad's family offered their home to stay, which was very kind and reflects the Nepali spirit.

The trip had been better than any tonic or medication. This place got me in a right frame of mind to be a success. I urge anyone going through crisis or tragedy to go away and volunteer.

Like the sign at school said:

'Open your mind not your mouth, I'm having a good day, don't mess it up!

Chapter 34
Long trip back to 'Kathmandon't'

Bang, bang, bang! There was a loud clattering knock on my door. I could see the corrugated metal door almost caving in under the weight of a fist. Bloody hell, the Grandad could had a strong knock for a old guy. I opened the door bleary eyed; my alarm hadn't gone off yet.

It was only 6am!

"We get the bus now," said Grandad.

"Are you serious? It's only 6am!" I said, half asleep, half irritated.

I was told I was going at 9am the day before but apparently the bus leaves at 7am, so I was really angry as it meant I wouldn't get to say bye to the boys. I hurriedly brushed my teeth, had a wash and put my clothes on. I was freezing outside, and I could feel the cold concrete floor against my bare feet.

I went out of my room and snuck into the small boys' bedroom.

"Bye bye, boys," tears welling up as I said it.

I know it was selfish to wake them, knowing they had a full day of school ahead.

I didn't get the warm send-off I was expecting. In fact, half of the boys looked annoyed I'd interrupted their sleep. Some of them hugged me and said bye, and the others stayed in bed, mainly Anil, Habir, and Ridesh. They weren't bothered in the slightest. Hadn't I touched their hearts in the same way they'd touched mine? Surprisingly it was the two older boys who came and hugged me and said *'thank you Mother, we will miss you'*. I'd really bonded with them.

The boys had a lifetime of being left and I guess I was just another transient person in their lives. In the short time I'd been there those six young men had changed me and they didn't have a clue. I didn't have the means to support them at that time, but I was determined to support them, and others like them.

The bus ride home I shared a ride with the old Grandad, Asim's Father, who tried to read my palm. To be honest he was actually really irritating me, and I just wanted to sit alone with my thoughts.

He said;

"You have a short little finger, you are destined for an unhappy life, just like Susila."

In my head, I thought, 'what a load of bollocks! I'm alright thanks'.

I hope Susila gets a second chance at happiness. She's so young and no one deserves to be put on the scrap heap at such a young age. I was fourteen years older than her and was determined not to be cast aside. The rest of the journey was long and excruciating, sat next to Grandad asking me questions about my family, my husband. Not content with trying to test my mind for three days at the orphanage with endless puzzles and maths games, he goes and invades my space by taking up too much room on the bus.

He was annoying me, but I knew he was just trying to be kind. The old guy was ok really, and the boys told me they liked him.

It seems you are only defined by what your husband does for work. It was easier to pretend and stop any more questions.

"Who is looking after your daughter?"

"What is your husband's job?"

230

"Does your father work? What is his job?"

"Is it well paid?"

"What is your home like?"

I wanted to scream: 'I'm a fucking strong, independent woman and I don't need a man to define me. My home is beautiful and its mine, not my husbands. I had a wonderful job and I was well paid. However, none of that bloody matters if you're miserable and unhappy with life, sometimes a simple life is better, easier'.

But I didn't. I sat there half answering his ridiculous questions and pretending to be some dumb stepford wife who was there on her husband's permission. I couldn't say a thing, I was staying at his family home in Kathmandu and didn't fancy a night on the streets. Four hours into the journey, I bumped into Santosh, the guy I met New Year's Eve at a truck stop in the middle of a mountain, how weird. After the clear views and normal roads in Pokhara I'd forgotten that some of the roads in Kathmandu were a mess, the bus ride back took nine hours. I arrived at Asim's and in 360 degree whirlwind journey I was back on the edge of Kathmandu with Everest as my backdrop and lovely Nani making me a cup of tea once again.
Asim and his lovely family do genuinely care and have been helping families for years. I was proud to have contributed to their team for a short time. I'd love to see more people helping out on his projects.

I couldn't be bothered with the rigmarole of getting a shower, but I wasn't sure if Emirates airlines and the Dubai Sheraton would let me in looking and smelling like a tramp. I'd had four showers in two and half weeks, and my hair hadn't seen a brush since Christmas Day. I wasn't quite looking Dubai glam. More of a hybrid between the old and new me; the self-styled 'white collar hippy'.
I couldn't wait for a nice hot shower and bath, and a lie down on a nice soft mattress.

At the Sheraton in Dubai I ran the bath and put far too many bubbles in and lay there soaking my grimy body. As I emerged myself in the warm, sweet smelling water I felt relaxed. My mind was at peace and my body felt soothed – I thought I might never get out.

I took out the small amount of make-up I had that was lurking in the bottom of my ruck sack for this moment. I had arranged to have drinks with a few friends I knew out in Dubai.
I'd saved a black lacy vest top, pencil thin black trousers, and tucked away my kitten heel black sling-backs at the bottom of my rucksack. Putting them on I felt awkward and not me anymore, the trousers were a bit baggier than they had been before my trip. I was so used to wearing walking clothes and fleeces; they'd become part of my new style.

On my way out I picked my phone off my bed, and a little message popped up and made my day;

"Hi Mom! We miss you."

Thanks, Tika for sending that, you made your 'Mother' very happy.

Chapter 35
Going Home

I arrived at Birmingham airport and was back where I had started. I half expected to have visitors greeting me with boards saying 'Welcome Home' but it was late and I knew Dad was at mine with Sophia.

My other friends probably couldn't remember when or where I was arriving.

The air was cold and once again it was wet and grey. For the second time in as many days I felt like Dorothy in the Wizard of Oz returning home after a wonderful adventure, only to find nothing had changed and no one really knew I was missing, a slight anti-climax as I was bursting with stories to tell everyone.

My journey was well and truly over, but the memories will last a lifetime. It was only a short break, but it did more for me than spending Christmas and New Year alone in the U.K.

I won't miss the traffic, the smog of Kathmandu, the snotting and phlegm hacking or the smell of the toilets.

I will miss the scenery, mountains, the heart and generosity of people, the walking, my coffee by the lake. I'll even miss the Daal Baat twice a day, and I will especially miss my boys.

Thank you to all the people I met along the way, who helped make my journey memorable.

Alex Ronald Sabelli and girlfriend who I met in the train station in Delhi. I might see you in Rome at some point.

To the lovely Belgian family who bought the boys ice cream and told me I was doing a good thing. The French / Dutch girls were working for the U.N. who I thought were doing an admirable thing. The two Scottish ladies who were working on a dental project, who educated me on the dental hygiene practise in rural Nepal.

To Pradeep, Alan Reed and family, I'll be back soon. Asim and his lovely family and project team Yubaraj and Susila, Grandad, and crazy Santosh.

More importantly to six amazing, cheeky and unique boys and the dog Sheru who have taught me more than I've ever learnt before. I'm glad I was the only volunteer, that made it more special for me.

I was exhausted and stressed before I came. I tried my best with the boys even if at times I felt about ninety years old trying to climb the hills and run after them. Thank you so much you made me so happy to be your 'Mother'! I miss you all.

Tika
Ramesh
Anil
Habir
Ridesh
Samil (Sammii, my baby).
I hope to see Kiran when I come back too.
Love you all, and I'll see you soon.

At the beginning of the trip someone told me Nepal stands for:

Nepal
Everlasting
Peace
And
Love

It really does!

I'd been home a few weeks and was re-adjusting to life when I received a message;

"Hi Dingbat, how are you? How was Nepal?"

234

It was Liam.

"It was amazing, in fact life changing." I replied.

"I'm very proud of you, you know that, don't you?" He replied.

"Thanks x"

I looked at the text for a while and a sense of achievement wafted across my body.
There it was. Finally, my compliment. In truth I was proud of what I'd done myself. I didn't need his or anyone's validation anymore, I was finally proud of me. I wasn't looking at someone else to tell me I was great or special, I knew I was. I know I didn't do anything remarkable and it's possible for anyone to work on a project.
I put the phone down and deleted Liam's number, I blocked him on social media and took away any opportunity he had to contact me. I didn't need him anymore.
I had a difficult situation, and instead of wallowing in self-pity I got up and did something, something for a group of people who haven't had the same privileges I've had. Finally, I no longer felt like the washed up school Mum whose husband had left her.

Epilogue
Forgiveness

Spending time with the boys made me appreciate that people make mistakes, we are all human, and underneath we are fundamentally the same. There are usually driving forces behind people's behaviour; whether that be good or bad.

Some of the boys had at least one parent. But due to being widowed, new marriages, poverty, too many children, or having to work away, they could no longer care for them. The boys were tossed aside due to circumstances beyond their control. The boys felt no resentment; they just got on with life and happy to take on its rollercoaster.

Being in Nepal had widely changed my perspective on things, and all the things I took for granted and thought was important became less so.

I tried to keep the vegan diet, I bought lentils and vegetables and stocked up on herbs and spices. I tried various recipes, and Daal Bat became my friend, although Sophia thought it was disgusting. I talked about the wonders of the Nepali diet which I'd found boring while there, but back home in Staffordshire seemed wonderfully exotic at least for a few weeks until hunger pangs came, and my old habits crept in.

I bagged up all the clothes that no longer fit me, or I hadn't worn in a year or so and took them to the charity shop. I toyed with selling the £600 Louboutin's and Mulberry handbags as their relevance had waned, but I'd had such a great night in them, and they appeared to be a symbol of my previous life. Like a trophy depicting my selfish, materialistic old self.

I smiled and knew there was more to me than having sex with random men and showing off in pair of expensive shoes. I'd come so far but knew there was still work to be done. In fact, the hardest work was yet to come.

All the things I'd accumulated or sought after in past 13 years had been just '*things*'. Things that weren't important and if you were to break them down to their functions;

Just clothes - to keep you warm.

Just food - to keep you fuelled.

Just work - to keep you financially secure.

Only marriage - provide a family and emotional dependence.

I was no longer angry with Steve for what he had done and how he had behaved. I was grateful for giving me our beautiful Daughter and pushing me to work hard. Steve had instilled a work ethic in me that would stay forever. His negative 'can't do' energy, exhausting as it was, made me more determined to succeed.
I had moved on mentally at least, and was at peace with the situation, knowing that the divorce was imminent and an end to the anguish was in sight.
He would have to deal with his decision and actions for the rest of his life and although he would never admit it, I knew he had regrets. I wasn't hanging around to argue and fight anymore.
It was his battle and his demons to deal with, on his own. That was all in the past and my future wouldn't include him.

As for Liam, we are not in touch anymore, at least for the foreseeable future. He has a girlfriend now and they seem pretty serious, so I'm not going to hang around and ruin that for him.
I'm grateful that he helped me forget about Steve and encouraged me to change.
He didn't actually do a great deal for me emotionally, and the power I had was always within me. However, I wouldn't have taken the journey without his input, or without trying to show off and impress him. Becoming obsessed with him and rejected by him as painful as it

was made me get over the Steve heart break quicker. While I was away, I realised that I'd replaced one form of suffering for another. If I look back at our friendship, I made all the same mistakes I had done with Steve. I wanted him to love me, to tell me I was amazing. I was desperate.

Liam was my strength test; he was brought to me to help me see I didn't need anyone, and I could do it alone.

I love him to pieces in the most heartfelt of ways. He's capable of so many wonderful things, and I hope one day he releases his fears and past hurts to realise them. I hope he realises his own self-worth, as I have mine.
I wish him well and hope he has a happy life and wish that one day we can sit and drink coffee as friends again, no judgement, no arguments and no seeking validation. Our relationship was a complex one; I loved him deeply on so many levels. He was my inspiration, my best friend and counsellor, but it was never meant to be.
For now, all three of us have different journeys to follow, and despite the heartache, unrequited love and conflict. one thing is for sure' I'm a lot richer for having had them in my life.

The Guru told me in Nepal,

"This had to happen, you couldn't carry on/ It had to end so you could cleanse your soul and go on your next journey. Your life is destined for better things, different things, you'll know what I mean in time."

My soul is more cleansed, and I think I do know what he meant now.

Taken from website: https://fractalenlightenment.com

"The capacity to be alone is the capacity to love. It may look paradoxical to you, but it's not. It is an existential truth: only those

people who are capable of being alone are capable of love, of sharing, of going into the deepest core of another person—without possessing the other, without becoming dependent on the other, without reducing the other to a thing, and without becoming addicted to the other. They allow the other absolute freedom, because they know that if the other leaves, they will be as happy as they are now. Their happiness cannot be taken by the other, because it is not given by the other."
~ Osho

Your strength comes from your ability to adapt and overcome falling apart and coming back together again, from wholeness to brokenness and back to a stronger better you.

What Next?

Watch out for my further tours, inspired blogs, and comical travel tips.

The journey has only just started for me.

Sophia and I have agreed to stick a pin in a map and plan the next trip.

So far, we've shortlisted:

- Istanbul for a food and drink tour.
- Costa Rica for a trip with Sophia.
- Argentina, I've always wanted to go.

I will go back to Nepal to see my boys and take Sophia to meet her adopted brothers. Nepal will always be in my heart as it was the first real trip that made me think about changing my perspective.

About the author

This is the first book by a Elise Kaye it's a semi autobiographical account of her travel to Nepal, some of the accounts are true but some are embellished for artistic purposes. She writes a regular eclectic blog on mental health, travel and occasionally education general ramblings.
Since returning from her trip she has re-trained as a clinical hypnotherapist and public speaking coach. She is a media spokesperson for several narcissistic abuse causes, encouraging others to tell their stories.